Foundations of Government and Public Administration

Series Editors
Jos C. N. Raadschelders
Ohio State University
Columbus, USA

R. A. W. Rhodes
University of Southampton
Southampton, UK

This series explores the values and ideals that ground a society at large and the nature of the various relations between society and government. Organised around three overarching themes—Great Thinkers about Government's Role and Position in Society, Foundations of Public Administration: Approaches to Studying Government, and Foundations of Government: Core Concepts and Ideas—the series will analyse government at its constitutional and foundational level. Such an approach is not yet mainstream, with public administration scholars more commonly focusing on the specific challenges, methods, skills, policies, and organizational structures of government's operations. This series will address that trend by providing a conceptual map of these fundamentals and making new knowledge and approaches relevant for understanding government accessible to readers by helping them to grasp their origins, meaning and relevance.

More information about this series at
http://www.palgrave.com/gp/series/15900

Daniel Little

A New Social Ontology of Government

Consent, Coordination, and Authority

Daniel Little
University of Michigan-Ann Arbor
Ann Arbor, MI, USA

ISSN 2523-7624   ISSN 2523-7632   (electronic)
Foundations of Government and Public Administration
ISBN 978-3-030-48922-9   ISBN 978-3-030-48923-6   (eBook)
https://doi.org/10.1007/978-3-030-48923-6

© The Editor(s) (if applicable) and The Author(s), under exclusive license to Springer Nature Switzerland AG 2020
This work is subject to copyright. All rights are solely and exclusively licensed by the Publisher, whether the whole or part of the material is concerned, specifically the rights of translation, reprinting, reuse of illustrations, recitation, broadcasting, reproduction on microfilms or in any other physical way, and transmission or information storage and retrieval, electronic adaptation, computer software, or by similar or dissimilar methodology now known or hereafter developed.
The use of general descriptive names, registered names, trademarks, service marks, etc. in this publication does not imply, even in the absence of a specific statement, that such names are exempt from the relevant protective laws and regulations and therefore free for general use.
The publisher, the authors and the editors are safe to assume that the advice and information in this book are believed to be true and accurate at the date of publication. Neither the publisher nor the authors or the editors give a warranty, express or implied, with respect to the material contained herein or for any errors or omissions that may have been made. The publisher remains neutral with regard to jurisdictional claims in published maps and institutional affiliations.

Cover illustration: © Melisa Hasan

This Palgrave Pivot imprint is published by the registered company Springer Nature Switzerland AG
The registered company address is: Gewerbestrasse 11, 6330 Cham, Switzerland

Acknowledgments

Several colleagues at the University of Michigan have been especially helpful to me as I worked my way through these ideas about social ontology and organizational theory, including Jason Owen-Smith, Elizabeth Armstrong, and James Wells. Raphael van Riel and his colleagues at the *Institut für Philosophie* at the Universität Duisburg-Essen provided a hospitable and productive environment for research and writing in January 2019, as well as very stimulating and formative discussion of several parts of the manuscript in seminars hosted at the *Institut für Philosophie*. Francesco Di Iorio and his colleagues in the School of Philosophy at Nankai University offered warm collegiality and helpful comments on several chapters of the manuscript during a productive visit to Nankai University, and also gave me a sense of how these issues may play out in China. Discussions about social causation at the University of Milan School of Public Policy and Governance with Alessia Damonte, Fedra Negri, and Flaminio Squazzoni have helped me formulate my ideas about social ontology more adequately. I also greatly appreciate ongoing conversations and seminars with George Steinmetz, Phil Gorski, Doug Porpora, Tim Rutzou, and Frédéric Vandenberghe about the ontological assumptions of critical realism. I received very helpful and astute comments on parts of the manuscript from students in a graduate course at the Ford School of Public Policy in fall 2019, including especially Zhibin Ye. I would like to extend special thanks to Jos Raadschelders, for both his invitation to contribute this volume and his extensive and helpful comments on the penultimate version of the manuscript. Finally, I am grateful to the University of Michigan-Dearborn for sabbatical support and other research support during 2018–2019 which allowed me the opportunity to spend time and energy on this book, and to the Ford School of Public Policy for the welcoming environment it has offered me.

PRAISE FOR *A NEW SOCIAL ONTOLOGY OF GOVERNMENT*

"Daniel Little challenges the traditional conception of government as consisting of layers and branches by defining it as the aggregated actions of hundreds of thousands of individuals assigned to roles, embedded in authority relations, and situated in cultures. Those actors pursue a mixture of private and public goals with limited agency within a complex assemblage of organizations that includes networks of authority, power, and collaboration. Little's reframing of what constitutes our government has profound implications for how we increase our democratic voices and how we design institutions singly and jointly to improve government performance."
—Scott Page, *Professor of Management and Organizations, Williamson Family Professor of Business Administration, Stephen M Ross School of Business, University of Michigan, USA*

"Daniel Little once again provides proof of the fruitfulness of an approach that is sensitive to both philosophical theory and social science models. Starting from a subtle version of an actor-centered social ontology, he presents an impressive, unified, and up-to-date account of the complex workings of government. This easily accessible, masterly crafted book will become an essential reference for philosophers and social scientists alike. In this up-to-date account of the complex workings of government, Daniel Little, leading figure in the philosophy of the social sciences, provides proof that the interaction between social ontology and social science can be extremely fruitful. This easily accessible book is bound to become a key text for all those interested in the nature of government, in social ontology, and in the explanatory power of realist interpretations of social science models."

—Raphael van Riel, *Senior Lecturer, Institute for Philosophy, Universität Duisburg-Essen, Germany*

"This delightful book assembles diverse organizational, social, and philosophical theories to address a burning contemporary question: on what grounds can we make social scientific claims about the character, workings and systematic dysfunctions of government? Little's well-crafted argument from social ontology illuminates new conceptual tools whose use yields a provocative reframing of how we talk about, think about, analyze and explain government."

—Jason Owen-Smith, *Executive Director, Institute for Research on Innovation & Science and Professor of Sociology, University of Michigan, USA*

Contents

1	Ontology and Government	1
2	Scientific Realism and the Study of Government	17
3	The Ontology of Composition	35
4	Intellectual Tools for Understanding Government	53
5	Institutions, Norms, and Networks	71
6	Sources of Organizational Failure	91
7	Electoral Democracy	111
8	What Does Government Do?	125
9	Governments as Regulators	145

10 Concluding Observations	161
References	165
Index	175

List of Figures

Fig. 8.1 Governmental action (*Source* Author) 132
Fig. 8.2 Environmental protection (*Source* Author) 137
Fig. 8.3 Banning DDT (*Source* Author) 138

CHAPTER 1

Ontology and Government

Abstract What kind of things do we need to hypothesize when we refer to "government"? A government is made up of actors—individuals who occupy roles; who have beliefs, interests, commitments, and goals; and who exist within social relations and networks involving other individuals both within and outside the corridors of power. How are the actors who make up government tied together through constraints, actions, institutions, values, incentives, norms, identities, emotions, and interests? What forms of social causation and influence serve to constitute the organizations and institutions of government? Recent work in organizational sociology has provided new tools for describing social arrangements within organizations on the basis of which organizations function. Current studies of organizations also provide a basis for understanding the importance and sources of dysfunction within government and other ensembles of organizations. This chapter lays the ground for developing an extensive theory of the social realities that constitute a modern government.

Keywords Actor-centered sociology · Government agency · Organization theory · Social ontology · Strategic action field

© The Author(s) 2020
D. Little, *A New Social Ontology of Government*,
Foundations of Government and Public Administration,
https://doi.org/10.1007/978-3-030-48923-6_1

Overview

What kind of things are we talking about when we refer to "government"? What sorts of processes, forces, mechanisms, structures, and activities make up the workings of government? In recent years philosophers of social science have rightly urged that we need to better understand the "stuff" of the social world if we are to have a good understanding of how it works. In philosophical language, we need to focus for a time on issues of *ontology* with regard to the social world. What kinds of entities, powers, forces, and relations exist in the social realm? What kinds of relations tie them together? What are some of the mechanisms and causal powers that constitute the workings of these social entities? Are there distinctive levels of social organization and structure that can be identified? Earlier approaches to the philosophy of the social sciences have largely emphasized issues of epistemology, explanation, methodology, and confirmation, and have often been guided by unhelpful analogies with positivism and the natural sciences. Greater attention to social ontology promises to allow working social scientists and philosophers alike to arrive at a more nuanced understanding of the nature of the social world. Better thinking about social ontology is important for the progress of social science. Bad ontology breeds bad science.

These issues are especially interesting when we consider the nature and role of "government" in the modern world. What is government? How does it work? How are the many actors and subjects of government tied together through constraints, actions, institutions, values, incentives, norms, identities, emotions, and interests?

The book seeks to provide a basis for a better understanding of some of the central puzzles of empirical political science: how does "government" express will and purpose? What accounts for both plasticity and perseverance of political institutions and practices? How do political institutions come to have effective causal powers in the administration of policy and regulation? And how can we arrive at a better understanding of the persistence of dysfunctions in government and public administration—failures to achieve public goods, the persistence of self-dealing behavior by the actors of the state, and the apparent ubiquity of the influence of private interests even within otherwise high-functioning governments?

If we are to think seriously about the ontology of government, it is good to begin with a few obvious ontological truths. Most basically, it is plain that any specific government is not one unitary thing. Instead, it is a composite thing that encompasses many social functions, networks, doings, and powers, at multiple and overlapping levels. Government is not precisely layered in the fashion suggested by an organizational chart. Rather, it consists of multiple systems, organizations, groups, specialists, brokers, and rogues working sometimes with considerable independence and sometimes with great coordination and subordination.

Consider some of these examples of the face of government, and notice the great heterogeneity they represent: the policeman on the beat, the health inspector, the city health department, the state and federal revenue services, the National Science Foundation, the state economic development agency, the mayor's office, the elected school board, the Nuclear Regulatory Commission, the President, and so on ad infinitum. There are ties among these nodes, both formal and informal, and there are sometimes organization charts that display functional relationships, authority structures, and flows of information along various offices and actors. But there is also substantial contingency and path dependence in the development of these institutions and relationships and a quilt-like arrangement of jurisdictions and histories.

Another important truth about government is that it is made up of actors—individuals who occupy roles; who have beliefs, interests, commitments, and goals; who exist within social relations and networks involving other individuals both within and outside the corridors of power; and whose thoughts, intentions, and actions are never wholly defined by the norms, organizational imperatives, and institutions within which they operate. Government officials and functionaries are not robots, defined by the dictates of role responsibilities and policies. So it is crucial to approach the ontology of government from an "actor-centered" point of view, and to understand the powers and capacities of government in terms of the ways in which individual actors are disposed to act in a range of institutional and organizational circumstances. Whether we think of the top administrators and executives, or the experts and formulators of policy drafts, or the managers of extended groups of specialized staff, or the individuals who receive complaints from the public, or the compliance officers whose job it is to ensure that policies are followed by insiders and outsiders—all of these positions are occupied by individual actors who bring their own mental frameworks, interests, emotions, and knowledge to the work they do in government.

This point is all the more important when we consider the range of tasks performed by government. Governments make decisions through legislation and executive agencies; they gather knowledge about complex challenges, both scientific and social; they set priorities for government itself, and indirectly for the society in which they operate; they establish policies and rules; they collect taxes; they wage war; and, of course, they seek to implement the rule of law and the scope and effectiveness of rules and policies. Generally, these tasks require extended processes of collaboration, delegation, coordination, and communication within the organizations that make up the divisions of government. And often enough these processes misfire, leading to outcomes that are counter-productive for both government and society.

Every part of this long list of tasks involves deep complexities that are of interest to political scientists and public administration specialists. And all of these activities involve the coordinated (or sometimes uncoordinated) activities of legions of individual actors. The workforce of the Environmental Protection Agency is over 14,000 men and women, and the Food and Drug Administration is comparable in size; the Department of Justice employs over 110,000 individuals in dozens of major departments and offices; the Department of Homeland Security employs 229,000 individuals and consists of over a dozen large sub-agencies and sub-bureaus. The Nuclear Regulatory Commission, a relatively small Federal agency with a very important and complex charge, has 3800 employees.

Now think of the possibilities of overlap, interference, and inconsistency that exist among the functionings and missions of diverse agencies. Each agency has its mission and priorities; these goals imply efforts on the part of the leaders, managers, and staff of the agency to bring about certain kinds of results. And sometimes—perhaps most times—these results may be partially inconsistent with the priorities, goals, and initiatives of other governmental agencies. The Commerce Department has a priority of encouraging the export of US technology to other countries, to generate business success and economic growth in the United States. Some of those technologies involve processes like nuclear power production. But other agencies—and the Commerce Department itself in another part of its mission—have the goal of limiting the risks of the proliferation of technologies with potential military uses. Here is the crucial point to recognize: there is no "master executive" capable of harmoniously adjusting the activities of all departments so as to bring about the best outcome for the country, all things considered. There is the President of the United States, of course, who wields authority over the cabinet secretaries who serve as chief executives of the various departments; and there is the Congress, which writes legislation charging and limiting the activities of government. But it is simply impossible to imagine an overall master executive who serves as symphony conductor to all these different areas of government activity. At the best, occasions of especially obvious inconsistency of mission and effort can be identified and ameliorated. New policies can be written, memoranda of understanding between agencies can be drafted, and particular dysfunctions can be untangled. But this is a piecemeal and never-complete process.

Recent work in organizational sociology has provided new tools for describing social arrangements within organizations and institutions. Richard Scott and Gerald Davis's major work *Organizations and Organizing* (2007) provides an excellent contemporary framework for understanding the workings of organizations, emphasizing rational, natural, and open-systems approaches to organizations. Their analysis sheds a great deal of light on the workings of government agencies. The word "organizing" in the title of their book signals the idea that organizations are no longer looked at as static structures within which actors carry out well defined roles, but are instead dynamic processes in which active efforts by leaders, managers, and employees define goals and strategies and work to carry them out. And the "open-system" phrase highlights the point that organizations always exist and function within a broader environment—political constraints, economic forces, public opinion, technological innovation, other organizations, and today climate change and environmental disaster.

This is a perfect place for application of Fligstein-McAdam strategic action field theory (Fligstein and McAdam 2012). Government is well conceived as interlinked action networks with tighter and looser linkages and strategic actions by a variety of actors. (Think of the jurisdictional struggles between FBI and state and local police authorities.) The theory of assemblages is another suggestive theory of social ontology in this context. Manuel DeLanda spells out some of the details of this ontological framework on the social world (2006). The social ontology of assemblage illuminates the modular and contingent arrangement of offices, networks, and actors that make up government at a period in time. Some of Marx's theories about politics and government are relevant as well—the salience of class interest in the formulation and application of government policy is plainly an important aspect of the ontology of government, in the United States and all other countries. And recent discussions of generativity and emergence offer new ways of thinking about the relations between higher level and lower level social entities. Subsequent chapters will introduce the reader to these theories and more.

WHAT DOES GOVERNMENT DO?

What does government do? In brief, government is the organized, formal, and normatively grounded expression of the common will of citizens and the public good of all of society (Rousseau). Government exercises a monopoly of coercive force in society on behalf of the legitimate goals of government (Weber). As Jos Raadschelders observes, "In the past 100-150 years, government has grown to become a complex service-providing and policy-developing institution the size of which has no historical precedent" (2013: 1). Government establishes a framework of law and policy within which society functions. Key functions of government include administration of justice and protection of individual liberties and rights; foreign diplomacy and military defense; provision for public goods and services; provision of social insurance and social welfare; and establishment of regulations to ensure public health and safety against externalities of private activity. Some laws and policies serve simply to establish the "rules of the game" through which ordinary life is carried out, including protection of civil and economic rights, procedures for conflict resolution, and laws of liberty and property. Other laws and policies are aimed at remedying current problems faced by society. The War on Poverty was President Lyndon B. Johnson's effort to create processes of social and economic change that would end severe poverty in the United States. The Civil Rights Act and the Voting Rights Act were aimed at eliminating racial discrimination in public and social life in the United States. The environmental legislation of the 1960s and 1970s was aimed at halting and reversing the decline of environmental quality witnessed in mid-twentieth-century in the United States and the adverse effects on public health and quality of life that ensued. Decades-long efforts to reform the way that healthcare insurance is provided to Americans eventually led to passage of the Obama administration's Affordable Care Act—with years of subsequent efforts by political actors in the opposition party to undo the policy.

Governments formulate policies in service of their priorities. A policy is a set of actions designed to bring about a set of social outcomes—improve air and water quality, decrease automobile accident fatalities, end child malnutrition. Policies—the action plans of government—may be the result of legislation or executive action through the workings of various governmental agencies, and both types processes raise interesting issues. The implementation of policy requires the ability of government to secure appropriate behavior by citizens and government officials alike; this challenge is the topic of Chapter 9 where we consider how government exerts its will.

Setting policy unavoidably involves gathering data about the processes in question and arriving at estimates of the range of effects various possible interventions are likely to have. And given that policies involve issues where there is a significant degree of risk and uncertainty, it is inevitable that government policy-setting processes need to have some appropriate way of measuring uncertainty and balancing risks and benefits. This knowledge-gathering and assessment process is also a key process of government and is discussed in a later chapter.

Much of the work of government is performed by agencies through policies, actions, and administration that have important effects on the interests and wishes of citizens and private organizations and corporations. Governmental agencies have rule-setting powers and powers of enforcement, delegated by Congress to permit them to carry out their assigned missions—the Federal Emergency Management Agency, the Environmental Protection Agency, the Food and Drug Administration, or the Social Security Administration. Agencies implement policies under broad enabling legislation enacted by Congress. They are generally large hierarchical organizations incorporating layers of administrators and technical experts, and the eventual content of a new policy is often the highly complex result of myriad different scientific assessments, interests, and voices. This is a key focal point for a theory of the ontology of government and a key point of application of current thinking in organizational sociology.

ACTOR-CENTERED SOCIAL ONTOLOGY

The social ontology we will explore here depends on an important premise, an approach to social thinking that can be described as "actor-centered." The basic idea is that social phenomena are constituted by the actions of individuals, oriented by their own subjectivities and mental frameworks and relationships with others. Higher-level institutions, organizations, and forces exist; but their properties and dynamics are constituted by the collective actions of the actors who make them up. It is recognized, of course, that the subjectivity of the actor does not come full-blown into his or her mind at adulthood; rather, we recognize that individuals are "socialized"; their thought processes and mental frameworks are developed through myriad social relationships and institutions. So the actor is a socially constituted individual (Little 2006, 2016). I refer to this conception of the social world as "methodological localism", according to which socially constituted and socially situated individual actors make choices within a set of locally instantiated norms, rules, social relationships, and opportunities.

Actor-centered social science begins in the intuition that social processes are embodied in the interactions of socially constructed individuals, and it takes seriously the idea that actors have complex and socially transmitted mental schemes of action and representation. So actor-centered sociologists are keen not to over-simplify the persons who constitute the social domain of interest. This means that they are generally not content with sparse abstract schemata of actors like those that pervade most versions of rational choice theory (Green and Shapiro 1994).

This assumption about the nature of the social world can be described as ontological individualism (Epstein 2009). It embodies the idea that there is no mysterious social "stuff" that is distinct from the actions and mental frameworks of the individuals who make up the social world. Ontological individualism does not force us to adopt the much stronger claims of methodological individualism (the idea that social explanations need to be reduced to statements about individuals). Rather, we are encouraged to recognize that individuals themselves are affected by social arrangements and relationships in the past and the present, so that the individual who plays a role in a social institution is herself "socially constituted" by past experience and learning in social environments. This point does not contradict the premise of an actor-centered approach to social science, because all of those earlier social experiences and interactions were themselves created by socially constructed individuals.

The idea of the "microfoundations" of a given social fact or entity reflects this view of the actor-centered nature of social entities (Little 1998, 2015, 2017). If we want to assert that a given social-level fact persists, we need to have some account of what features of the local environment of action would induce independent actors to choose actions in ways that contribute to the emergence and persistence of the social fact in question. The properties and causal powers of government require microfoundations.

Organizations as Social Things

A key concept in analyzing the workings of government is the idea of an organization. Organizations exist on a range of scales, from a small business to an architectural firm to a university to a government agency. Examples of organizations include things like the University of Chicago, the Department of Energy, the Baltimore police department, a collective farm in Sichuan in 1965, the operations staff of a nuclear power plant, a large investment bank on Wall Street, an NGO such as Oxfam, and the Xerox Corporation. It does not make sense to think of government itself as a single organization, because it is evident from what has been said already that a government is an ensemble of many organizations, loosely connected through a variety of means. But understanding how mid-size organizations work will be crucial to allowing us to analyze the nature of government action, knowledge formation, and decision.

An organization is a meso-level social structure. It is a structured group of individuals, often hierarchically organized, pursuing a relatively clearly defined set of tasks. Scott and Davis (2007) describe an organization in these terms: "Most analysts have conceived of organizations as social structures created by individuals to support the collaborative pursuit of specified goals. Given this conception, all organizations confront a number of common problems: all must define (and redefine) their objectives; all must induce participants to contribute services; all must control and coordinate these contributions; resources must be garnered from the environment and products or services dispensed; participants must be selected, trained, and replaced; and some sort of working accommodation with the neighbors must be achieved" (Scott and Davis 2007: 23).

In the abstract, an organization is a set of norms, rules, procedures, and roles that regulate and motive the behavior of the individuals who function within the organization in pursuit of the organization's goals. There are also informal practices within an organization that are not codified that have significant effects on the functioning of the organization (for example, the coffee room or cafeteria as a medium of informal communication). Some of those individuals have responsibilities of oversight, which is a primary way in which the goals and rules of the organization are transformed into concrete patterns of activity by other individuals. Another behavioral characteristic of an organization is the set of incentives and rewards that it creates for participants in the organization. Often the incentives that exist were planned and designed to have specific effects on behavior of participants; by offering rewards for behaviors X, Y, Z, the organization is expected to produce a lot of X, Y, and Z. Sometimes, though, the incentives are unintended, created perhaps by the intersection of two rules of operation that lead to a perverse incentive leading to W.

An important characteristic of recent organizational theory has to do with the way that theorists think about the actors within organizations. Instead of looking at individual behavior within an organization as being fundamentally rational and goal-directed, primarily responsive to incentives and punishments, organizational theorists have come to pay more attention to the non-rational components of organizational behavior—values, cultural affinities, cognitive frameworks and expectations. This approach does not disregard the aspect of goal-directed purposiveness, but it recognizes that action and choice are motivated by a broad palette of considerations that matter to the individual actor.

Charles Perrow pays a great deal of attention to the ways that actors choose their courses of action within organizations (1999 [1984], 2014 [1974]). Central to his account is the idea of bounded rationality and the limits on rational planning and decision-making within an organization, an approach that derives from the theories of Herbert Simon and James March (Simon 1997; March and Simon 1958). Perrow emphasizes the inherent diversity of goals and purposes that are operative within an organization at any given point. He describes the "garbage can" theory of organizational goal-setting and problem-setting (2014: 135). Executives, managers, and other decision-makers are portrayed as unavoidably opportunistic, in the sense that they address one set of problems rather than another without a compelling reason for thinking that this is the best path forward for the organization. "Goals may thus emerge in a rather fortuitous fashion, as when the organization seems to back into a new line of activity or into an external alliance in a fit of absentmindedness" (135). Associated with this idea is the idea advanced by March and Simon that plans and goals are often adopted retrospectively rather than in advance of action. "No coherent, stable goal guided the total process, but after the fact a coherent stable goal was presumed to have been present. It would be unsettling to see it otherwise" (135).

This recognition of the multiplicity and sketchiness of organizational goals casts some doubt on the rationalism and functionalism that theorists sometimes bring to organizations (the idea that organizations possess the structures and goals they need to optimize the achievement of their goals). Perrow specifically endorses these doubts, "emphasizing instead the accidental, temporary, shifting, and fluid nature of all social life" (2014: 136, 137).

Perrow's considered theory of organizations also emphasizes an interpretation of organizations as vehicles of *power* through which some individuals control the behavior and products of others (2014: 259). Power is exercised within organizations, and it is also exercised in application to competitors in the broader environment of action. He articulates this view clearly in *Organizing America* (2002), where he argues that one of the primary social uses of the legal corporation is to serve as a vehicle for the wielding of power by the owners of concentrated wealth (2002: 1–2).

Contemporary organizational theory gives a great deal of emphasis to culture and mental frameworks in its theory of the organizational actor. Scott and Davis describe organizational culture in these terms: "culture describes the pattern of values, beliefs, and expectations more or less shared by the organization's members" (Scott and Davis 2007). This focus leads to another important shift of emphasis in current ideas about organizations, involving an emphasis on informal practices, norms, and behaviors that exist within organizations. Rather than looking at an organization as a rational structure implementing mission and strategy, contemporary organization theory confirms the idea that informal practices, norms, and cultural expectations are ineliminable parts of organizational behavior.

It is apparent that an organization needs to have a *functional structure* in which the activities of individuals or departments carry out specialized tasks. These sub-units depend upon the high-level work of other departments or individuals, and the functional structure of the organization can be more or less appropriate to the task. The organization succeeds to the extent that its component parts succeed in identifying the needs and opportunities facing the organization and in carrying out their roles in responding to those needs and opportunities. Poor performance in one department can have the effect of ruining the overall success of the organization to carry out its mission—even if other departments are highly successful in carrying out their tasks. Charles Perrow highlights this kind of organizational deficiency in *Normal Accidents: Living with High-Risk Technologies* (1999 [1984]).

Another important variable in bringing about organizational effectiveness concerns the procedures within the organization that are designed to encourage high-quality effort and results on the parts of the individuals who occupy roles throughout the organization. One line of response to this issue flows through a system of supervision and assessment. This approach emphasizes observation of performance and establishment of positive and negative incentives to motivate satisfactory performance. Supervisors are tasked to ensure that employees are exerting themselves and that their work product is of satisfactory quality. However, supervision by itself is insufficient. Herbert Simon (1997 [1947]) emphasizes that a crucial role of administrative leadership is the task of motivating the employees of the organization to carry out the plan efficiently and effectively. Simon notes that supervision by itself is insufficient to elicit high-quality performance; instead he highlights formal authority (enforced by the power to hire and fire), organizational loyalty (cultivated through specific means within the organization), and training as key organizational factors leading to high-quality performance by actors within an organization.

The complexity of an organization stems from the fact that a number of different kinds of activities are being carried out simultaneously by different groups of people, and there is no authoritative single "master bureaucrat" who sets tasks and oversees results for all agents of the organization. Inevitably there is an unavoidable degree of decentralization of activity, with decision-makers at a variety of levels who are empowered to set the agendas of their units in such a way as to best achieve the overall goals of the organization. And higher-level leaders have a responsibility for attempting to achieve a suitable degree of collaboration and communication among lower-level leaders to make it likely that the activities of the units will contribute to a coherent and effective effort to achieve the organization's goals. Moreover, complex organizations that fail to achieve a sufficient degree of coordination of effort internally wind up being unsuccessful; their product is often one that reflects the specific needs of each of the units, but fails to satisfy the overall goals of the organization.

The idea of *a principal-agent problem* is highly relevant within organizations at every level. The executive wants the supervisor to faithfully perform his/her tasks of supervision. But since the executive does not directly monitor the performance of the supervisor, it is possible for the supervisor to shirk his/her duties and permit faulty performance by those he supervises. Likewise, the supervisor expects that the operator will continue to monitor and control the machine throughout the day; but it is possible for the operator to keep a solitaire window open on the screen.

Each level of accountability, then, requires both formal expectations and a basis for trust in the good faith of the participants in the organization. These facts of organizational behavior will be considered more fully in Chapter 6.

The quality and focus of leadership is generally taken to be an important factor in the performance of an organization. The central tasks of an organization's leaders include a number of responsibilities. Leaders help set the strategic direction for the organization; they implement actions and processes at unit-levels within the organization; they collaborate with each other in efforts to achieve higher effectiveness within and across units; they seek out opportunities for new activities or initiatives that will further one or more priorities for the organization. And, as anyone knows who has worked within a variety of organizations—both organizations and leadership groups function at a very wide range of effectiveness, from the dysfunctional to the superb.

Another facet of organizational performance plainly has to do with *internal communication, coordination, and collaboration.* The eventual success or failure of an organizational initiative will depend on the activities of individuals and units spread out throughout the organization. The work of various of those units can be made more effective or less effective by the ease and seriousness with which they are able to communicate with each other. Suppose an automotive company is designing a new model. Many units will be involved in bringing the design to fruition. If the body designers, the power train designers, and the manufacturing engineers have not talked to each other, there is a likelihood that solutions chosen by one set of specialists will create major problems for the other specialists. Thomas Hughes provides an excellent analysis of the organizational characteristics of the design process used in the United States military aerospace sector in the 1950s and 1960s in *Rescuing Prometheus: Four Monumental Projects That Changed the Modern World* (1998).

What does this discussion of organizations tell us about the ontology of government? A great deal. Scott and Davis (2007) emphasize several key "ontological" elements that any theory of organizations needs to address: the environment in which an organization functions; the strategy and goals of the organization and its powerful actors; the features of work and technology chosen by the organization; the features of formal organization that have been codified (human resources, job design, organizational structure); the elements of "informal organization" that exist in the entity (culture, social networks); and the people of the organization. These features shed light on government organizations and agencies as much as they do corporations and non-profit organizations. To understand the workings of the Department of Energy we need to investigate the environment within which it operates (governmental, private-sector actors, scientific community, universities); we need to know what the official and actual goals of the agency are; we need to know who its primary actors are; we need to know how the work of the agency is organized and managed; and we need to know quite a bit about the informal practices and social networks that exist within the agency and between agency staff and other actors.

More generally, this survey of organizational studies reinforces the importance of taking an actor-centered approach to understanding the workings of government. Second, it provides a basis for asserting that governments have causal properties, both internally (affecting the activities of other governmental agencies) and externally (affecting the outcomes and behavior of citizens, consumers, and economic and political actors outside of government). It gives us an important indication of how to proceed with the task of investigating the workings of government: consider specific agencies and departments in terms of the mission and priorities assigned to them; the effectiveness of executive management of the agency; the effectiveness of the processes through which work is done, incentives are assigned, and information is developed and shared.

Finally, current empirical and theoretical studies of organizations provide a very strong basis for understanding the importance and origins of dysfunction within government and other ensembles of organizations. We now have a vocabulary for dissecting and analyzing the workings of the organizations that make up government.

References

DeLanda, Manuel. *A New Philosophy of Society: Assemblage Theory and Social Complexity*. London; New York: Continuum International Publishing Group, 2006.
Epstein, Brian. "Ontological Individualism Reconsidered." *Synthese* 166 (2009): 187–213.
Fligstein, Neil, and Doug McAdam. *A Theory of Fields*. New York: Oxford University Press, 2012.

Green, Donald P., and Ian Shapiro. *Pathologies of Rational Choice Theory: A Critique of Applications in Political Science*. New Haven: Yale University Press, 1994.
Hughes, Thomas Parke. *Rescuing Prometheus*. 1st ed. New York: Pantheon Books, 1998.
Little, Daniel. *Microfoundations, Method and Causation: On the Philosophy of the Social Sciences*. New Brunswick, NJ: Transaction Publishers, 1998.
Little, Daniel. "Levels of the Social." In *Handbook for Philosophy of Anthropology and Sociology*, edited by Stephen Turner and Mark Risjord, 15, 343–71. Handbook of the Philosophy of Science. Amsterdam; New York: Elsevier Publishing, 2006.
Little, Daniel. "Supervenience and the Social World." *Metodo* 3, no. 2 (2015): 125–45.
Little, Daniel. *New Directions in the Philosophy of Social Science*. London: Rowman & Littlefield Publishers, 2016.
Little, Daniel. "Microfoundations." In *The Routledge Companion to Philosophy of Social Science*, edited by Lee McIntyre and Alex Rosenberg. London; New York: Routledge, 2017.
March, James G., and Herbert A. Simon. *Organizations*. New York: Wiley, 1958.
Perrow, Charles. *Normal Accidents: Living with High-Risk Technologies—With a New Afterword and a Postscript on the Y2K Problem*. Princeton, NJ: Princeton University Press, 1999 [1984].
Perrow, Charles. *Organizing America: Wealth, Power, and the Origins of Corporate Capitalism*. Princeton, NJ: Princeton University Press, 2002.
Perrow, Charles. *Complex Organizations: A Critical Essay*. 3rd ed. Brattleboro, VT: Echo Point Books and Media, 2014 [1972].
Raadschelders, Jos C. N. *Public Administration: The Interdisciplinary Study of Government*. Paperback Edition. Oxford; New York: Oxford University Press, 2013.
Scott, W. Richard, and Gerald F. Davis. *Organizations and Organizing: Rational, Natural, and Open System Perspectives*. 1st ed. Upper Saddle River, NJ: Pearson Prentice Hall, 2007.
Simon, Herbert A. *Administrative Behavior: A Study of Decision-Making Processes in Administrative Organizations*. 4th ed. New York: Free Press, 1997 [1947].

CHAPTER 2

Scientific Realism and the Study of Government

Abstract When we discuss government we refer to social entities, forces, and relations like these: organization, agency, social network, cultural scheme, social actor, normative system, institution, and local culture. The fundamental question of social ontology raised here is this: what kinds of entities, powers, and causal influence do we need to postulate in order to have an adequate theory of government? To take these questions seriously, we must be realists in the philosophical sense: we must assume that there is a reality underlying the observable characteristics of the thing we are investigating. Scientific realism is the view that developed areas of science offer theories of the nature of the real things and properties that underlie the observable world, and that the theories of well-confirmed areas of science are most likely approximately true. The chapter introduces the reader to the central ideas of scientific realism in application to the social sciences.

Keywords Scientific realism · Critical realism · Causal mechanism · Causal power · Social causation · Morphogenesis

The central topic of this book is the ontology of government, a philosophical exploration of the entities and causal powers that underlie the workings of government. To take the question of social ontology seriously, we must be realists in the philosophical sense: we must assume that there is a reality underlying the observable characteristics of the thing we are investigating. In particular, I will maintain that we ought to be scientific realists. We should work on the premise that one of the goals of scientific study of a domain is to discover the real, underlying entities, forces, powers, and relations that make it up and give rise to its observable characteristics. And we are justified in believing that the hypotheses about unobservable social entities made by successful social theories in a given domain of social life are likely to be approximately true.

Scientific realism is the view that developed areas of science offer theories of the nature of the real things and properties that underlie the observable world, and that the theories of well-confirmed areas of science are most likely approximately true (Boyd 1990; Harré 1970; Bhaskar 1975, 1989; Manicas 2006; Porpora 2015; Little 2016). According to scientific realists, science provides knowledge about reality independent from our ideas and theories; and the methods of science justify our belief in these representations of the real world. (Ilkka Niiniluoto's *Critical Scientific Realism* is a detailed and rigorous recent treatment of the doctrine of scientific realism; Niiniluoto 1999.)

Here is how Peter Manicas summarize his interpretation of scientific realism:

> Theory provides representations of the generative mechanisms, including hypotheses regarding ontology, for example, that there are atoms, and hypotheses regarding causal processes, for example, that atoms form molecules in accordance with principles of binding. We noted also that a regression to more fundamental elements and processes also became possible. So quantum theory offers generative mechanisms of processes in molecular chemistry. Typically, for any process, there will be at least one mechanism operating, although for such complex processes as organic growth there will be many mechanisms at work. Theories that represent generative mechanisms give us understanding. We make exactly this move as regards understanding in the social sciences, except that, of course, the mechanisms are social. (75)

This is a good representation of the position commonly taken by philosophers towards the question of scientific realism, in the social sciences no less than in the natural sciences. Realism has to do with discovering underlying processes that give rise to observable phenomena. And causal mechanisms are precisely the sorts of underlying processes that are at issue.

In this chapter we will examine the main outlines of the theory of scientific realism as it applies to the social realm. We will also look at several specific ontological assumptions: persistent social structures, features of mentality embedded within a social process, and the idea that there are concrete social causal mechanisms that lead to change at both observable and unobservable levels of government.

REALISM FOR SOCIAL SCIENCE

What is involved in taking a realist approach to the social world? Most generally, realism involves the view that at least *some* of the assertions of a field of social knowledge—sociology, economics, political science, anthropology—make true statements about the properties of unobservable social things, processes, and states in the domain of study. Scientific realism raises important questions when we apply it to the social sciences. For one thing, it requires rigorous efforts at conceptual clarification as social scientists formulate ideas about underlying social realities. For example, if we postulate that "class" is an important entity or structure in the modern world, we need to have a clear formulation of what we mean by the concept of class, and how its objectivity in the social world can be validated. In fact, sociological theories of social class depend upon concrete research efforts that have been performed to identify, specify, and investigate the workings of class. Conceptual specification is crucial: we need to know what a given researcher means to encompass in his or her use of the term "class structure", and how empirical evidence can be gathered to shed light on the phenomena of class. When a social theory of class is put forward, we must ask detailed questions about its content and intended implications. Is it a claim about the exercise of power; about social attitudes at the individual level; about the mechanisms of opportunity and selection; about the differential assignment of privilege; about modes of speech and thought; or about the arrangements in society that reproduce the distinctions of class?

What features of social-science research justify us in believing that some theories in the social sciences succeed in identifying real unobservable social entities? There is, of course, the familiar "argument to the best explanation," itself a version of the hypothetico-deductive method of inference. We are justified in believing theories for which there is an adequate range of successful deductive application to the world of observation. But second, there is a very different kind of argument for social realism that is not commonly available in the natural sciences: the piecemeal investigation of claims and theories about social entities, properties, and forces. If we believe that class conflict is a key factor in explaining political outcomes, we can do sociological research to further articulate what we mean by class and class conflict, and we can investigate specific social and political processes to piece together the presence or absence of these kinds of factors.

So it seems that we can justify being realists about class, field, *habitus*, market, coalition, ideology, organization, value system, ethnic identity, institution, and charisma, without relying exclusively on the hypothetico-deductive model of scientific knowledge upon which the "inference to the best explanation" argument depends. We can look at sociology and political scienceas loose ensembles of empirically informed theories and models of meso-level social processes and mechanisms, each of which is to a large degree independently amenable to empirical investigation. And this implies that social realism should be focused on mid-level social mechanisms and processes that can be identified in the domains of social phenomena that we have studied rather than sweeping concepts of social structures and entities.

The fundamental question of social ontology when applied to the study of government is this: what kinds of entities, powers, and causal influence do we need to postulate in order to have an adequate theory of government? Consider this list of substantive concepts often used in describing government and its structures and powers: organization, authority, social network, communication, normative system, organizational culture, mental framework, public good, private and public interest, institution, structure, trust. Are these real things in the social realm? Do theories of government succeed in identifying real underlying features of the social world when they offer specific ideas about how governments function? And is it possible to arrive at a manageable list of entities and powers that will suffice?

When we discuss government action and the realities of government functions, we refer to entities, forces, and relations like these: organization, agency, social network, cultural scheme, social actor, normative system, institution, and local culture. Moreover, we believe that these items "really" exist in the workings of government, and that they convey effects on other elements of government. These statements presuppose the existence of social entities like organizations, professional culture, and the financial interests and influence of big business. And they make the assumption that these underlying entities and properties have causal powers that produce both stability and change within the structures in which they exist. The question for social ontology is to assess whether these assumptions made by theorists of government and public administration about the underlying workings of this limited aspect of government are plausible and whether they are empirically and theoretically supportable.

Specific Strands of Social Realism

Here are several specific ways in which scientific realism is relevant in the social sciences. They all have to do with the kinds of statements in the social sciences that can be interpreted as expressing facts about the social world, independent of our theories and concepts.

Causal realism. We can be realist about the assertions about causation and causal mechanisms. There is such a thing as social causation. Causal realism is a defensible position when it comes to the social world: there are real causal relations among social factors (structures, institutions, groups, norms, and salient social characteristics like race or gender). We can give a rigorous interpretation to claims like "racial discrimination causes health disparities in the United States" or "rail networks cause changes in patterns of habitation". It is justified to take the position that there is a fact of the matter as to whether X caused Y in the circumstances, and we can assert the objective reality of social causal mechanisms. On the realist interpretation, social causal mechanisms exist in the social world— they are not simply constructs of the observer's conceptual scheme. And the statement that "Q is the process through which X causes Y" makes a purportedly objective and observer-independent claim about Q; it is an objective social process, and it conveys causation from X to Y. Q is the causal mechanism underlying the causal relationship between X and Y. These facts serve to explain the appeal that investigative methods such as Mill's methods, random controlled trials, field experiments, and quasi-experiments have for social-science researchers. Researchers are attempting to assess causal hypotheses about the relations that exist among discrete social factors by observing circumstances in which those factors are present or absent.

Structure realism. We can be realist about the existence of extended social entities and structures—for example, "the working class," "the American Congress," "the movement for racial equality," or "the Department of Energy." These social entities and structures have some curious ontological characteristics—it is difficult to draw boundaries between members of the working class and the artisan class, so the distinctness of the respective classes is at risk; institutions like the Congress change over time; a social movement may be characterized in multiple and sometimes incompatible ways; and social entities don't fall into "kinds" that are uniform across settings. But it is justified to think that the Civil Rights movement was an objective fact in the 1960s or that the Congress exists and is a partisan environment. And this is a version of social realism.

Social-relations realism. If we say that "Pierre is actively involved in a network of retired French military officers", we refer to a set of social relations encapsulated under the concept of a social network and composed of many pair-wise social relations. Here too we can take the perspective of social realism. It seems unproblematic to postulate the objective reality of both the pair-wise social relations and the aggregate network that these constitute. Each level of social relationship can be investigated empirically (we can discover that Pierre has regular interactions with Jean but not with Claude), and it seems unproblematic to judge that there is a fact of the matter about the existence and properties of the network—independent of the assumptions and concepts of the observer.

Meaning realism. Now, how about the hardest case: meanings and the objectivity of interpretation. Can we say that there is ever a fact of the matter about the interpretation of an action or thought? When Thaksin offends Charat by exposing the bottoms of his feet to him—can we say that "Charat's angry reaction is the result of the meaning of this insulting gesture in Thai culture"? Even here, it is credible that there is a basis for saying that this judgment expresses an objective fact (even if it is a fact about subjective experience); and therefore, we can interpret this sentence along realist lines: "Thaksin's gesture was objectively offensive to Charat in the setting of Thai culture." It is evident that many of our interpretations of behavior and action are substantially underdetermined by context and evidence; so it may be that much interpretation of meaning does not constitute a "fact of the matter." But this seems to be a fact about particular judgments rather than a universal feature of the interpretation of meanings.

These examples make it clear that it is reasonable to take a realist perspective on many of the assertions and theories of the social sciences; and this implies that we can interpret social science statements as being approximately true of a domain of social phenomena that have objective properties (i.e. properties that are independent from our conceptualization of them).

In short, we can justify being realists about many of the core social-scientific concepts that have been used by social scientists in a range of disciplines: for example, market, coalition, ideology, organization, value system, ethnic identity, institution, class, field, habitus, and charisma without apology. We can look at sociology and political science as loose ensembles of empirically informed theories and models of meso-level social processes and mechanisms, each of which is to a large degree independently verifiable. And this implies that social realism should be focused on mid-level social mechanisms and processes that can be identified in the domains of social phenomena that we have studied rather than sweeping concepts of social structures and entities.

CRITICAL REALISM

A particularly influential version of scientific realism in the social sciences is the theory of critical realism put forward by Roy Bhaskar and others (Bhaskar 1975; Archer 1995, 1998; Elder-Vass 2010). This approach is deliberately developed as a post-positivist and anti-Humean framework for the philosophy of science. Bhaskar and others reject David Hume's theory of causation as "regular succession" of events. Instead, they argue that causation depends upon the real and often unobserved causal powers of the constituents of the world. Significantly, the Humean theory of causation underlies much methodological thinking in the social sciences, including statistical analysis of data to discover causal relations among factors. Instead, the goal of the social sciences is to use theoretical and observational methods to discover the real properties of underlying social entities and the real characteristics of the social mechanisms that produce change in the social world. Critical realism endorses the central thesis of scientific realism—that there is a distinction between observation and the underlying reality of things, and that a key goal of science to discover the hidden properties of the world. Bhaskar rejects the naïve empiricism of earlier theories of science, according to which the sole content of science was its ability to consolidate and explain patterns of observations. Instead, he argues that the role of science is to provide theories of the unobservable entities, powers, and structures whose characteristics generate the observations we make of the world.

It is entirely open to a critical realist, of course, to make use of the methods of statistical analysis and inquiry in seeking out the causal relations that exist within a domain of phenomena. Realists reject the view that evidence of statistical regularities and correlations represent the full story of causation; but they do not reject the idea that a given set of underlying processes should be expected to give rise to a set of correlations and associations. Bhaskar's point is rather an ontological one: the reality of a causal relation is to be found in the real underlying "generative causal mechanisms" that are at work, not the regularities themselves. At the same time, however, it is entirely legitimate for empirical scientists to seek out causal relationships through the regularities these underlying causal mechanisms should be expected to produce. Realism begins with ontology, but it extends very logically to a variety of methods of inquiry, both quantitative, comparative, and qualitative.

Central to Bhaskar's theory of causation is his conception of things and powers:

> The world consists of things, not events. Most things are complex objects, in virtue of which they possess an ensemble of tendencies, liabilities and powers. It is by reference to the exercise of their tendencies, liabilities and powers that the phenomena of the world are explained. Such continuing activity is in turn referred back for explanation to the essential nature of things. On this conception of science it is concerned essentially with what kinds of things they are and with what they tend to do; it is only derivatively concerned with predicting what is actually going to happen. (Bhaskar 1975: 41)

So things possess real causal powers, and we explain the behavior of objects (and ensembles) as a consequence of the operation of their powers. Further, causal mechanisms gain their active quality through the powers embodied in the entities of which they consist. Critical realism gives priority to the challenge of discovering concrete causal mechanisms which lead to real outcomes in the natural and social world. (See Archer et al. [2016] for an accessible statement of the key assumptions of critical realism.)

The idea of "generative causal mechanisms" is a core element of critical realism. Bhaskar and other philosophers of science in the tradition of critical realism place great emphasis on this idea. Here is Bhaskar's description of the idea.

> There is nothing esoteric or mysterious about the concept of the generative mechanisms of nature, which provide the real basis of causal laws. For a generative mechanism is nothing other than a way of acting of a thing. It endures, and under appropriate circumstances is exercised, as long as the properties that account for it persist. (pp. 41–42)

What does Bhaskar have in mind in applying these ideas to the social realm? Critical realism proposes an approach to the social world that pays particular attention to objective and material features of the social realm—property relations, impersonal institutional arrangements, supraindividual social structures. Between structure and agent, critical realism seems most often to lean towards structures rather than consciously feeling and thinking agents. Bhaskar offers examples throughout his work of enduring social items like social structures, social class, economic forces, and relations of political power. Equally, however, we can postulate the reality of more ideational social entities—ideologies, mental frameworks, locally embodied cultures and normative systems, and the like. For each of these kinds of entities we can provide an account of how they work that is grounded in socially constituted individual actors and the institutions in which they find themselves.

Take for example the idea of a social identity. A social identity seems inherently subjective. It is the bundle of ideas and frameworks through which one places himself or herself in the social world, the framework through which a person conceptualizes his/her relations with others, and an ensemble of the motivations and commitments that lead to important forms of social and political action. All of this sounds subjective in the technical sense—a part of the subjective and personal experience of a single individual. It is part of consciousness, not the material world. So it is reasonable to ask whether there is anything in a social identity that is available for investigation through the lens of critical realism. The answer seems to be fairly clear. Ideas and mental frameworks have social antecedents and causal influences. Individuals take shape through concrete social development that is conducted through stable social arrangements and institutions. Consciousness has material foundations. And therefore, it is perfectly appropriate to pursue a realist materialist investigation of social consciousness. This was in fact one important focus of the Annales school of historiography (Burguière 2009).

This is particularly evident in the example of a social identity. No one is born with a Presbyterian or a Sufi religious identity. Instead, children, adolescents, and young adults acquire their religious and moral ideas through interaction with other individuals, and many of those interactions are determined by enduring social structures and institutional arrangements. So it is a valid subject of research to attempt to uncover the pathways of interaction and influence through which individuals come to have the ideas and values they currently have. This is a perfectly objective topic for social research.

But equally, the particular configuration of beliefs and values possessed by a given individual and a community of individuals is an objective fact as well, and it is amenable to empirical investigation. The research currently being done on the subcultures of right wing populism illustrates this point precisely. It is an interesting and important fact to uncover (if it is a fact) that the ideologies and symbols of hate that seem to motivate right wing youth are commonly associated with patriarchal views of gender as well.

So ideas and identities are objective in at least two senses, and are therefore amenable to treatment from a realist perspective. They have objective social determinants that can be rigorously investigated; and they have a particular grammar and semiotics that need to be rigorously investigated as well. Both kinds of inquiry are amenable to realist interpretation: we can be realist about the mechanisms through which a given body of social beliefs and values are promulgated through a population, and we can be realist about the particular content of those belief systems themselves.

These considerations seem to lead to a strong conclusion: critical realism can be as insightful in its treatment of "subjective" features of social consciousness and identities as it is in study of objective social structures.

Mechanisms and Powers

At the core of much thinking about scientific realism in application to the social world is the idea of a causal mechanism. Thinkers as diverse as Roy Bhaskar (1975) and Peter Hedström (2005) agree that causation is ontologically real, and that causation works through concrete causal mechanisms. So it is crucial for social scientists to uncover the *causal mechanisms* that underlie various social phenomena. To explain a social outcome or regularity, we need to provide an account of why and how it came about; and this means providing a causal analysis in terms of which the explanandum appears as a result. We can only assert that there is a causal relationship between X and Y if we can offer a credible hypothesis of the sort of underlying mechanism that connects X to the occurrence of Y. Social explanations should seek out the causal mechanisms that underlie the social phenomena of interest (Little 1991, 2011).

Causal mechanisms theory (CM) rests on the idea that events and outcomes are caused by specific happenings and powers, and it proposes that a good approach to a scientific explanation of an outcome or pattern is to discover the real mechanisms that typically bring it about. It also brings forward an old idea about causation—no action at a distance. So if we want to maintain that class privilege causes ideological commitment, we need to be able to tell an empirically grounded story about how the first kind of thing conveys its influence to changes in the second kind of thing. (This is essentially the call for microfoundations.) Causal mechanisms theory is more basic than other theories of causation, in that it provides a further explanation for findings produced by other methods. Once we have a conception of the mechanisms involved in a given social process, we are in a position to interpret a statistical finding as well as a finding about the necessary and/or sufficient conditions provided by a list of antecedent conditions for an outcome.

Causal-mechanisms theory also suggests a different approach to data gathering and a different mode of reasoning from both quantitative and comparative methods. This approach is the case-studies method: identify a small set of cases and gain enough knowledge about how they played out to be in a position to form hypotheses about the specific causal linkages that occurred (mechanisms). This approach is less interested in finding high-level generalizations and more concerned about the discovery of the real inner workings of various phenomena. Causal mechanisms methodology can be applied to single cases (the Russian Revolution, the occurrence of the Great Leap Forward famine), without the claim to offering a general causal account of famines or revolutions. So causal mechanisms method (and ontology) pushes downward the focus of research, from the macro level to the more granular level.

On this approach, it is argued that it is essential to recognize that causal relations depend on the existence of real social-causal mechanisms linking cause to effect. The regularity-based theory of causation advocated by David Hume is rejected. Discovery of correlations among factors does not constitute the whole meaning of a causal statement. Rather, it is necessary to have a theory of the mechanisms and processes that give rise to the correlation. Moreover, it is defensible to attribute a causal relation to a pair of factors even in the absence of a correlation between them, if we can provide evidence supporting the claim that there are specific mechanisms connecting them. So mechanisms are more fundamental than regularities.

The discovery of social mechanisms often requires the formulation of mid-level theories and models of these mechanisms and processes—for example, the theory of free-riders. This is what Robert Merton had in mind when he introduced the idea of "sociological theories of the middle range": an account of the real social processes that take place above the level of isolated individual action but below the level of full theories of whole social systems (Merton 1963). Marx's theory of capitalism illustrates the latter; Jevons's theory of the individual consumer as a utility maximizer illustrates the former. Coase's theory of transaction costs is a good example of a mid-level theory (Coase 1988): general enough to apply across a wide range of institutional settings, but modest enough in its claim of comprehensiveness to admit of careful empirical investigation. Significantly, the theory of transaction costs has spawned major new developments in the new institutionalism in sociology (Brinton and Nee 1998).

The importance of this idea for social-science research is profound; it confirms the notion shared by many researchers that attribution of social causation depends inherently on the formulation of good, middle-level theories about the real causal properties of various social forces and entities.

What is a causal mechanism? Consider this formulation: a causal mechanism is a sequence of events, conditions, and processes through which the explanans produces the explanandum (Little 1991: 15). A causal relation exists between X and Y if and only if there is a set of causal mechanisms that connect X to Y. This is an ontological premise, asserting that causal mechanisms are real and are the legitimate object of scientific investigation. Mario Bunge (1997) and Jon Elster (1989) took similar positions, and James Mahoney (2001) provides a review of the multiple theories of causal mechanisms that have been advanced in the past twenty years. The view took a large step forward with the publication of Hedström and Swedberg's *Social Mechanisms: An Analytical Approach to Social Theory* (1998), and on the empirical research side with the publication of McAdam, Tarrow, and Tilly's *Dynamics of Contention* (2001).

Emphasis on causal mechanisms for adequate social explanation has several favorable effects on sociological method. It takes us away from uncritical reliance on uncritical statistical models. But it also may take us away from excessive emphasis on large-scale classification of events into revolutions, democracies, or religions, and toward more specific analysis of the processes and features that serve to discriminate among instances of large social categories (Tilly 1995).

Giving central emphasis on the task of discovering the causal mechanisms that produce or generate the outcomes we are interested in gives substantial support to the idea of methodological pluralism. There is no single method of inquiry that permits researchers to discover causal mechanisms. Properly understood, there is no contradiction between the effort to use quantitative tools to chart the empirical outlines of a complex social reality, and the use of theory, comparison, case studies, process-tracing, and other research approaches aimed at uncovering the salient social mechanisms that hold this empirical reality together.

There is a key intellectual obligation that goes along with postulating real social mechanisms: to provide an account of the substrate within which these mechanisms operate. This I have attempted to provide through the theory of methodological localism (Little 2006)—the idea that the causal nexus of the social world is constituted by the behaviors of socially situated and socially constructed individuals. To put the claim in its extreme form, every social mechanism derives from facts about institutional context, the features of the social construction and development of individuals, and the factors governing purposive agency in specific sorts of settings. And different research programs target different aspects of this nexus.

In Chapter 1 we explored a social ontology grounded in the actions and relations of socially constituted actors. This view of the social world is very powerful, in that it provides a broad account of how social causation works. Individuals have motivations, ideas, mental frameworks, values, and emotions; these individual characteristics are socially created through specific institutional and familial settings (which in turn have their own individual-level foundations); and individuals are socially situated within institutional settings involving rules, norms, and incentives. When individuals act within these settings they bring about specific kinds of outcomes. Or in other words, features of the institutional settings, when presented to specific kinds of actors, causally produce certain kinds of social outcomes.

This entails, basically, that we need to understand all higher-level social entities and processes as being composed of the activities and thoughts of individual agents at a local level of social interaction; we need to be attentive to the pathways of aggregation through which these local-level activities aggregate to higher-level structures; and we need to pay attention to the iterative ways in which higher-level structures shape and influence individual agents. Social outcomes are invariably constituted by and brought into being by socially constituted, socially situated individual actors. Both aspects of the view are important. By referring to "social constitution" we are invoking the fact that past social arrangements have created the social actor. By referring to "social situatedness" we invoke the idea that existing social practices and rules constrain and motivate the individual actor. So this view is not reductionist, in the sense of aiming to reduce social outcomes to pre-social individual activity.

We also want to refer to supra-individual actors—firms, agencies, organizations, social movements, states. The social sciences are radically incomplete without such constructs. But all such references are bound by a requirement of microfoundations: if we attribute intentionality to a firm, we need to be able to sketch out an account of how the individuals of the firm are led to act in ways that lead to the postulated decision-making and action.

Critical Realism and Morphogenesis

One of the most important thinkers to have introduced new ideas into the critical realism field is Margaret Archer. Several books in the mid-1990s represented genuinely original contributions to issues about the nature of social ontology and methodology, including especially *Realist Social Theory: The Morphogenetic Approach* (1995) and *Culture and Agency: The Place of Culture in Social Theory* (1996). Archer's work addresses several topics of interest here, including especially the agent-structure dichotomy. Anthony Giddens offers one way of thinking about the relationship between agents and structures (1979). Archer takes issue with the most fundamental aspect of Giddens's view—his argument that agents and structures are conceptually inseparable. Archer argues instead for a form of "dualism" about agents and structures—that each pole needs to be treated separately and in its own terms. She acknowledges, of course, that social structures depend on the individuals who make them up; but she doesn't believe that this basic fact tells us anything about how to analyze or explain facts about either agents or structures. Here is the opening paragraph of *Realist Social Theory*.

> Social reality is unlike any other because of its human constitution. It is different from natural reality whose defining feature is self-subsistence: for its existence does not depend upon us, a fact which is not compromised by our human ability to intervene in the world of nature and change it. Society is more different still from transcendental reality, where divinity is both self-subsistent and unalterable at our behest; qualities which are not contravened by responsiveness to human intercession. The nascent 'social sciences' had to confront this entity, society, and deal conceptually with its three unique characteristics. (Archer 1995: 1)

Archer argues that the two primary approaches that theorists have taken—methodological individualism and methodological holism—are both inadequate. They represent what she calls upward and downward *conflation*. In the first case, "society" disappears and is replaced by some notion of aggregated individual action; in the second case "agents" disappear and the human individuals do no more than act out the imperatives of social norms and structures. She associates the first view with J. S. Mill and Max Weber and the second view with Durkheim. On her view, agents and structures are distinct, and neither is primary over the other. She refers to her view as the "morphogenetic" approach. Here is how she explains this concept:

> The 'morpho' element is an acknowledgement that society has no pre-set form or preferred state: the 'genetic' part is a recognition that it takes its shape from, and is formed by, agents, originating from the intended and unintended consequences of their activities. (1995: 5)

Morphogenesis applies at all levels, from "the capitalist system" to "the firm" to "the actor" to personal identity and motivation. And she believes that properties at various levels—micro and macro—have a degree of autonomy from each other, which she refers to as "emergence".

So what is Archer's central notion, the idea of *morphogenesis*? It is the idea that processes of change occur for agents and social structures in interlocking and temporally complex ways. Agents are formed within a set of social structures—norms, language communities, power relationships. The genesis of the agent occurs within the context of these structures. On a larger time scale, the structures themselves change as a result of the activities and choices of the historically situated individuals who make them up. She summarizes this ontology as a set of cycles with different time frames: structural conditioning => social interaction => structural elaboration (1995: 16). This notion leads Archer to a conception of the social and the actor that reflects a fundamentally historical understanding of social processes. Formation and transformation are the central metaphors (1995: 154).

Archer's realist theory of morphogenesis is helpful for our central task here, coming to a better understanding of the social ontology of government. The idea that actors are socially constituted and socially situated is a different way of expressing her point that actors are constituted by surrounding social structures. The idea that structures are themselves adapted and changed by active individuals doing things within them corresponds to her "social interaction" and "structural elaboration" phases of morphogenesis. The methodological insight that seems to come along with morphogenesis—the idea that it is valuable to move both *upwards* towards more comprehensive social structures and *downwards* towards more refined understanding of action and interaction—is certainly a part of the view associated with current organizational sociology and actor-centered sociology. Her view of the inherent "transformability" of society (1) parallels the facts of the heterogeneity and contingency of social arrangements to be discussed in the next chapter. Finally, her notion that social ontology must be addressed before we can make much progress on issues of methodology and explanation seems right as well.

REFERENCES

Archer, Margaret Scotford. *Realist Social Theory: The Morphogenetic Approach*. Cambridge; New York: Cambridge University Press, 1995.

Archer, Margaret Scotford, ed. *Culture and Agency: The Place of Culture in Social Theory*. Rev. Cambridge, UK; New York, NY, USA: Cambridge University Press, 1996.

Archer, Margaret Scotford, ed. *Critical Realism: Essential Readings*. Critical Realism–Interventions. London; New York: Routledge, 1998.

Archer, Margaret S., Claire Decoteau, Philip Gorski, Daniel Little, Doug Porpora, Timothy Rutzou, Christian Smith, George Steinmetz, and Frederic Vandenberghe. "What Is Critical Realism?" *Perspectives* 38, no. 2 (2016): 4–9.
Bhaskar, Roy. *A Realist Theory of Science*. Leeds: Leeds Books, 1975.
Bhaskar, Roy. *The Possibility of Naturalism: A Philosophical Critique of the Human Sciences*. 2nd ed. London: Harvester Wheatsheaf, 1989.
Boyd, Richard. "Realism, Approximate Truth, and Philosophical Method." In *Scientific Theories*, edited by C. Wade Savage. Minneapolis: University of Minnesota Press, 1990.
Brinton, Mary C., and Victor Nee, eds. *New Institutionalism in Sociology*. New York: Russell Sage Foundation, 1998.
Bunge, Mario. "Mechanism and Explanation." *Philosophy of the Social Sciences* 27, no. 4 (1997): 410–65.
Burguière, André. *The Annales School: An Intellectual History*. Ithaca, NY: Cornell University Press, 2009.
Coase, R. H. *The Firm, the Market, and the Law*. Chicago: University of Chicago Press, 1988.
Elder-Vass, David. *The Causal Power of Social Structures: Emergence, Structure and Agency*. Cambridge: Cambridge University Press, 2010.
Elster, Jon. *Nuts and Bolts for the Social Sciences*. Cambridge: Cambridge University Press, 1989.
Giddens, Anthony. *Central Problems in Social Theory: Action, Structure and Contradiction in Social Analysis*. Berkeley: University of California Press, 1979.
Harré, Rom. *Principles of Scientific Thinking*. Chicago: University of Chicago, 1970.
Hedström, Peter. *Dissecting the Social: On the Principles of Analytical Sociology*. Cambridge, UK; New York: Cambridge University Press, 2005.
Hedström, Peter, and Richard Swedberg, eds. *Social Mechanisms: An Analytical Approach to Social Theory*. Studies in Rationality and Social Change. Cambridge, UK; New York: Cambridge University Press, 1998.
Little, Daniel. *Varieties of Social Explanation: An Introduction to the Philosophy of Social Science*. Boulder, CO: Westview Press, 1991.
Little, Daniel. "Levels of the Social." In *Handbook for Philosophy of Anthropology and Sociology*, edited by Stephen Turner and Mark Risjord, 15, 343–71. Handbook of the Philosophy of Science. Amsterdam; New York: Elsevier Publishing, 2006.
Little, Daniel. "Causal Mechanisms in the Social Realm." In *Causality in the Sciences*, edited by Phyllis Illari, Federica Russo, and Jon Williamson. Oxford: Oxford University Press, 2011.
Little, Daniel. *New Directions in the Philosophy of Social Science*. London: Rowman & Littlefield Publishers, 2016.

Mahoney, James. "Beyond Correlational Analysis: Recent Innovations in Theory and Method." *Sociological Forum* 16, no. 3 (2001): 575–93.

Manicas, Peter T. *A Realist Philosophy of Social Science: Explanation and Understanding.* Cambridge, UK; New York: Cambridge University Press, 2006.

McAdam, Doug, Sidney G. Tarrow, and Charles Tilly. *Dynamics of Contention.* New York: Cambridge University Press, 2001.

Merton, Robert K. "On Sociological Theories of the Middle Range." In *Social Theory and Social Structure*, edited by Robert K. Merton. New York: Free Press, 1963.

Niiniluoto, Ilkka. *Critical Scientific Realism.* Oxford; New York: Oxford University Press, 1999.

Porpora, Doug. *Reconstructing Sociology: The Critical Realist Approach.* Cambridge; New York, NY: Cambridge University Press, 2015.

Tilly, Charles. "To Explain Political Processes." *American Journal of Sociology* 100 (1995): 1594–1610.

CHAPTER 3

The Ontology of Composition

Abstract This chapter addresses ontological questions concerning the *composition* of social structures and entities, and their relationships to the actors who compose them. Our theories and ordinary language refer to governmental structures, institutions, and organizations at a range of levels: actors and officials, agencies, knowledge systems, social networks, and offices and bureaus. The philosophical position of ontological individualism maintains that all social phenomena are ultimately constituted by the social actors who make them up. However, the chapter also recognizes that we need to recognize the reality of higher-level social entities—institutions, normative systems, social identities, power relations, and social networks. The chapter argues that it is legitimate to postulate the existence of social entities; but it argues that social entities, forces, and conditions must have microfoundations at the level of the social actors who compose them. The chapter discusses the idea of a social actor as a socially constituted and socially situated individual with mental frameworks that guide his or her choices of action.

Keywords Agent-based models · Emergence · Generativism · Heterogeneity · Microfoundations · Ontological individualism

This chapter addresses several ontological questions concerning the *composition* of social structures and entities, and their relationships to the actors who compose them and the other structures among which they exist. When we discuss the workings of government and public administration we refer to governmental structures, institutions, and organizations at a range of levels of scope and causal powers: actors and officials, agencies, knowledge systems, social networks, and offices and bureaus located within various units of government. What can we say about how these various entities, processes, and levels of governmental authority relate to each other, and how they derive from the structured activities and mental frameworks of the actors who compose them? We will also consider the interesting question of the stability, plasticity, and heterogeneity of social structures and organizations and the implications these features have for an ontology of government.

Ontological Individualism and the Role of Microfoundations

What is the nature of the social world? And what is the nature of the actor in society? These are the fundamental questions for social ontology. *Ontological individualism* is a minimalist principle of ontology for our understanding of the social world. It is the view that ultimately, real human individuals are the "stuff" that constitutes all social entities, processes, and relationships. Through their thoughts and actions human beings constitute the properties and reality of social entities. We also need to recognize the existence of other social entities—institutions, normative systems, social identities, power relations, and social networks, for example. Postulating supra-individual social entities no more breaks the premise of ontological individualism than does postulating cells or cognitive systems break the premise of physicalism (the idea that ultimately everything in the physical world depends on the properties of atoms, physical forces, and sub-atomic physical reality).

However, the ontological premise of methodological individualism has a consequence for our hypotheses about higher-level social entities and forces, often expressed in terms of the idea of "microfoundations" (Little 1998, 2017). We can define this idea as a schematic description of the ways that properties, structural features, and causal powers of a social entity are produced and reproduced by the actions and dispositions of socially situated individuals. This view does not necessarily lead us to the position of methodological individualism. Methodological individualism is a view about social explanation that holds that social explanations must proceed from statements about the characteristics of individuals to conclusions about the properties of ensembles of individuals. This methodological constraint does not follow from ontological individualism, however, any more than the truth of physicalism entails that we need to derive the biological properties of a neuron from the properties of the fundamental particles that constitute it. It is entirely legitimate for social scientists to maintain that there are stable causal and structural properties that attach to some social entities, that can be investigated empirically, and that can be provided with simple but non-exact theories of corresponding microfoundations.

One way of motivating the requirement of microfoundations is to observe that it is a prescription against "magical thinking" in the social realm. There is no "social stuff" that has its own persistent causal and structural characteristics; rather, all social phenomena are constituted by patterns of behavior and thought of populations of individual human beings. And likewise, social events and structures do not have inherently social causal properties; rather, the causal properties of a social structure or event are constituted by the patterns of behavior and thought of the individuals who constitute them and nothing else.

This approach to social ontology gives central attention to the social actor. What is a "social actor"? In brief, actors are socially constituted and socially situated. Individual human beings are socially constituted in the most fundamental sense imaginable. Since birth we are exposed to social practices, norms, conventions, modes of interaction, aversions, preferences, and behaviors. Social life and the creation of social actors is an ongoing process. Through the process of evolution of our species, we have gained the neurophysiology necessary to permit us to learn the mental frameworks, practices, conventions, and language that surround us (Gibbard 1990). The process of development and maturation is one through which each individual builds a mental map of the world he or she inhabits and a rich vocabulary in terms of which to characterize that world. Likewise the individual builds a set of practical frameworks defining goals, purposiveness, and normative imperatives which guide his or her actions and choices. There is no such thing as the extra-social or pre-social individual. It is evident that those formative examples that are key to personal development come from other human individuals, likewise shaped and informed by their own histories of interaction with a previous generation. The individual is socially constituted—often in ways below consciousness, sometimes at a level where self-awareness and learning can alter the program. (This is the hope of emancipation from racism, sexism, and domination: the mental frameworks we have absorbed that all too often embody these features can be questioned and changed.) By the time an individual reaches adolescence and adulthood, he or she has internally embodied a stable set of normative, cultural, behavioral, and cognitive practices that serve as a grounding for action and choice in the social world.

The social actor is also socially *situated*. This phrase captures the basic structural fact that individuals find themselves within systems of rules, power relations, incentives, opportunities, social networks, and authority systems that influence their choices in a variety of ways. (a) The institutions and organizations within which the individual actor operates create opportunities, incentives, and disincentives for action which influence the behavior of the individual given his or her goals and desires. (b) Power and authority relations influence the range of choices available to the individual. (c) Relations of trust and loyalty provide inducements and confidence for pursuing some actions and avoiding other actions. (d) The normative and cultural commitments of the groups within which the actor lives give both positive and negative motivations for action. (e) The physical and infrastructural environment within which the actor lives encourages and facilitates certain choices and discourages other choices. Access to transportation makes involvement in a distant mass demonstration more convenient and therefore more likely.

Mark Granovetter (1985) introduced the idea of embeddedness to capture parts of both aspects of the social actor. The idea of an "embedded" individual is contrasted to the idea of an atomized actor; this implies that the individual's choices and actions are generated, in part anyway, by the actions and expected behavior of other actors. It is a relational concept; the embedded actor exists in a set of relationships with other actors whose choices affect his or her own choices as well. And this in turn implies that the choices actors make are not wholly determined by facts internal to their spheres of individual deliberation and beliefs; instead, actions are importantly influenced by the observed and expected behavior of others.

Some of Granovetter's discussion crystallizes around the social reality of *trust* within a system of economic actors. Trust is an inherently relational social category; it depends upon the past and present actions and interactions within a group of actors, on the basis of which the actors choose courses of action that depend on expectations about the future cooperative actions of the other actors. Trust for Granovetter is therefore a feature of social relations and social networks: "The embeddedness argument stresses instead the role of concrete personal relations and structures (or "networks") of such relations in generating trust and discouraging malfeasance" (1985: 490). And trust is relevant to cooperation in all its variants—benevolent and malicious as well. As Granovetter points out, a conspiracy to defraud a business requires a group of trusting confederates. So it is an important sociological question to investigate how those bonds of trust among thieves are created and sustained.

Now turn to the supra-individual social features that we find in our world—political parties, business firms, football teams and their supporters, charitable organizations, labor unions, universities, normative and cultural schemes, religious or ethnic identities. The current characteristics and behaviors of social institutions and other social entities are driven by the actions and thoughts of the individuals who constitute them at present. Further, institutions have characteristics that provide a degree of stability with respect to change of membership. The norms of behavior that are part of the current realities of a religious congregation are embodied in the mental frameworks of the members; deviants within the community will find that other members resist their efforts to defy the institution and its practices and commitments. Or consider corporate stability. The systems of oversight and audit that exist in a corporation were designed precisely to detect and control deviant behavior within the corporation. These systems themselves depend upon the willing participation of a number of individuals—auditors and supervisors—but their institutional roles have a degree of influence on their behavior as well.

Here is a formulation of a social ontology that captures these ideas about social actors and social structures.

- The social world exists as the embodiment of sets of individual persons with powers, capacities, and actions and interactions, and who stand in a vast range of concrete social relationships with each other.
- Social entities (structures, institutions, normative communities, shared meanings, social identities, organizations, networks) are composed of groups of individuals with specified features of mental frameworks, purposes, and actions.

Wherever we start our examination of the social world, from the situation of particular individuals, to labor unions, firms, and faith organizations, to federal agencies and multinational trading regimes, the logic of the social world seems to be the same: there are groups of actors planning and acting in that locus, these actors possess frameworks of thinking and acting that influence their behavior, there are structures and rules that surround them, and there are organizations and structures that constrain and motivate them. There is an up, down, and sideways everywhere in social action. Crucially for our purposes here, this is equally true in the zone of the institutions of government.

This view of the iterative and cyclical nature of social and individual action is parallel to Margaret Archer's (1995) theory of morphogenesis, discussed in Chapter 2. On her view, agents and structures are distinct and inseparable, and neither is primary over the other. It also resembles an innovative idea offered by James Coleman in his treatment of institutions and norms, where he describes these social ensembles as a "house of cards" in which the stability of the structure depends entirely on the interrelations that exist among the participants in reinforcing the architecture of the ensemble (1990: 43–44).

Emergence and Relative Explanatory Autonomy

A recurring topic in the philosophy of social science (and some other areas of philosophy, including philosophy of biology) is the idea of "emergence". Roughly speaking, this is the idea that higher-level entities in a particular domain have properties that are significantly different from the properties of the entities of which they are composed. More radically, it is sometimes maintained that some of the properties of higher-level entities cannot be derived from the properties of the composing units at all. The topic arises because virtually all the entities and forces that are of interest in the sciences are composite entities: they are composed of components arranged in particular ways which come together to create the properties of the whole. A molecule is composed of atoms connected by atomic bonds; an alloy is composed of a mix of metals in particular proportions; and a labor union is composed of leaders, members, and organizational resources. In each case it is reasonable to ask, how do the properties of the components influence the properties of the ensemble?

There are several logical possibilities concerning how parts and wholes may fit together. They include:

- *generativism*: the properties of the lower-level components and their arrangement *determine* the properties of the ensemble (Epstein 2006);
- *supervenience*: the properties of higher-level ensembles *depend* on the properties of the components (Kim 1993);
- *reductionism*: the properties of the higher-level can be reduced to or derived from facts about the properties and arrangement of the lower-level components (Wimsatt 2006; Boyd 1980);
- *weak emergence*: the properties of higher-level ensembles are different in kind and quality from the properties of the components (Elder-Vass 2010);
- *strong emergence*: the properties of higher-level ensembles are different in kind from the properties of the components and cannot be derived from full knowledge of the components (Bhaskar 1993);
- *computational emergence*: the properties of the higher-level ensembles are in principle generated by the properties of the components, but it is computationally impossible to derive the ensemble properties from the component properties (Simon 1962).

(A more extensive discussion of these possibilities is provided in Little [2016].)

Let us consider briefly whether the concept of emergence is of use in the social sciences. Is it the case that social institutions and structures such as the Food and Drug Administration or the Social Security Administration have properties that are importantly distinct from—perhaps to some degree independent from—the properties of the individuals who constitute these large organizations? Do the FDA or the SSA have emergent properties?

There are several features of the social world of organizations and institutions that justify an affirmative answer to the question. First, the properties of these large organizations are largely independent from the particular individuals who make them up. It is important that there is a director of audits in the FDA and a director of research; but whether that individual is Mr. Smith or Ms. Jones is immaterial to the actions and properties of the organization. So we can rightly say that the organization is largely independent from the particular properties of its constituent individuals (with occasional important exceptions). Moreover, large agencies and groups of agencies are complex systems in the technical sense that Miller and Page (2007) describe: there are feedback relationships and non-linearities that exist within them that make their eventual behavior difficult to predict. Moreover, the actors themselves are "adaptive": their behavior changes over time as they learn from experience (Morçöl 2012).

Second, we can certainly observe that organizations have properties and characteristics of action that are unintended by any of the participants, past or present. These are the "system" effects that organizations develop through the particular intersections of rules, practices, and divisions of labor that they have evolved over time. No one intended that the Federal Emergency Management Agency would fail in the spectacular ways in which it did during the Katrina crisis in 2005; its failure was structural and systemic rather than intended or designed. The failure derived from organizational dysfunctions that were embodied in the rules and practices of the organization. These failures were of course "acted out" by the individuals who performed their tasks within the organization; but a good explanation will seek out the source of the dysfunction rather than the particular pathways through which it manifested itself.

Third, it is plain that it is futile to attempt to explain or understand the full workings of a large and complex organization based solely on an account of the states of mind and agency of the individuals who make it up. This attempt would be roughly as pointless as would be the effort to predict tomorrow's weather by attempting to track the current states of all the molecules in the atmosphere and aggregating their interactions over a twenty-four-hour period. It is computationally impossible; but more importantly, it would not shed any light on the intermediate-level causal mechanisms that influence the weather (atmospheric pressure changes, water temperature across the ocean, evaporation processes, ...). This is the thrust of the position of "computational emergence" mentioned above.

Finally, it is credible to believe that there is "downward causation" within an extended system of institutions, organizations, and individual actors. Individuals constitute institutions; but institutions shape and influence individuals as well. Governments affect individuals by compelling compliance with the legal system; more indirectly they influence individuals through support for public education institutions. Governments contribute to the socialization of individuals, who in turn come to contribute to the causal operations of government. Moreover, we can identify pathways of influence laterally across organizations and institutions. The Department of Labor through its collection of unemployment statistics influences the kinds of decisions the Commerce Department makes when it comes to encouraging various kinds of economic development.

These points give some reason to support a view somewhat similar to the idea of emergence for the social world. Organizations have properties that are independent from the particular individuals who make them up, and they have causal properties which are effectual both with respect to individuals and to other organizations.

What these points do not support, however, is the strong version of the theory of emergence, the idea that there are properties of the social world that do not derive at all from the properties of the actors who make up the social world. (Advocates for this strong version of emergence include Bhaskar in some of his statements, Niklas Luhmann et al. [2013], and a few others.) Instead, we have very good reason to believe that all of the properties of an institution are embodied in the mental frameworks, expectations, and behaviors of the individuals who make up the space in which the institution operates. Individuals are shaped by an embodied set of institutions and practices at a point in time, and those institutions and practices are themselves embodied in the thoughts, actions, and meanings of an overlapping but distinct set of individuals.

Fortunately, we are not forced to choose between the radical extremes of methodological individualism and strong emergentism. Rather, we can recognize the importance of causal properties of entities at a range of levels, from micro to meso to macro, and to assert the "relative explanatory autonomy" of various of these levels. The idea of relative explanatory autonomy derives from debates about a parallel issue in the philosophy of psychology: do cognitive processes have properties that are independent from the properties of the neurophysiological systems that underlie them? Jerry Fodor (1974) argued that the "special sciences" could appropriately examine phenomena at an intermediate level of organization without being required to reduce their claims about higher-level facts into claims about foundational-level facts. Of course cognitive mechanisms must be grounded in neurophysiological processes. But this does not entail that cognitive theories need to be *reduced* to neurophysiological statements. This view can be referred to as the theory of *relative explanatory autonomy*. The key insight here is that there are good epistemic and pragmatic reasons to countenance explanations at a meso-level of organization, without needing to reduce these explanations to the level of individual actors. (These issues are taken up in Little [2016].)

So ontological individualism and actor-centered social science do not force us to become reductionists; instead it is scientifically and ontologically permissible to choose to focus on intermediate levels of social organization and attempt to uncover the causal properties and mechanisms that are at work at this level. The meso-level investigator acknowledges that the phenomena he or she is investigating have "microfoundations" at the level of individual actors; but the investigator also seeks to identify the relatively stable structures and causal relationships that exist at the intermediate level of organization.

Let us take stock on the composition problem. The most reasonable position seems to be the position of "relative explanatory autonomy". First, there is no reason to accept reductionism as a principle of scientific inquiry (Boyd 1980). It is perfectly legitimate to investigate the properties of higher-level entities and forces without attempting to derive their properties from lower-level constituents. In particular, it is legitimate to examine the properties of various kinds of organizations and agencies without being committed to deriving those properties from the nature and behavior of the actors who make them up. Second, the principle of generativism is plausible and is similar to the principle of ontological individualism. It is a recognition of the point that social things are ultimately composed of individuals in social relationships with each other, and equivalent to the idea that social entities rest upon microfoundations at the level of socially situated actors. Again, generativism does not entail methodological individualism (or the specific methodology of agent-based modeling). Third, the idea of weak emergence is acceptable as well; part of the fascination of social-science research is precisely the surprise we experience when we find that a social entity behaves differently than we might expect given what we know about the individuals who make it up. Likewise the idea of computational emergence is credible; it simply recognizes the fact, familiar from other areas of the sciences, that models of complex phenomena involving the behavior of millions or billions of elements are simply impossible to compute. The idea of strong emergence is not supportable, because it makes an irresolvable mystery of the workings of the higher-level domain. If social entities do not depend ultimately on the characteristics and behavior of the individual actors who compose them, then what do they depend upon? There appears to be no available answer. The position of relative explanatory autonomy with regard to social structures and mid-level social entities holds simply that we can investigate empirically the properties of various social structures and entities without being compelled to replace our investigations with a generative account of how the properties of a structure or institution are "generated" by the behaviors of the individuals who constitute it.

This means that organizational sociology and the study of government functioning can legitimately use a meso-level vocabulary in singling out the phenomena of interest for empirical study. It is perfectly appropriate to focus empirical attention on the organizational characteristics of a government agency, or the culture embodied in the workplace of that agency, or the normative schemes that regulate behavior within the workplace—without being obliged to trace the particular pathways through which individual characteristics embody those properties.

So the position recommended here is anti-reductionist and methodologically receptive to multi-level investigations of complex phenomena. It is a position that endorses ontological individualism (the view that the social world depends ultimately on the thoughts and actions of individual social actors) and that endorses as well the requirement of microfoundations. Claims about social entities need to be consistent with credible theories of how those features of the social entity may be embodied in the actions and mental frameworks of the actors. That said, it is perfectly reasonable and scientifically legitimate to attempt to discover the causal and systemic properties of intermediate-level social entities like organizations and government agencies.

PLASTICITY, PERSISTENCE AND CHANGE

Turn now to a second set of important ontological characteristics of social entities. The entities of the social world are different in deep ways from the entities of physics or chemistry. Social structures, value systems, cultures, practices, and networks are profoundly different from molecules or metals because their properties are not permanent and fixed over time. Social entities are *plastic* in their structures and properties. Second, different instances of various categories of social entities demonstrate substantial variation within the group. There is great *heterogeneity* within social categories. We know roughly what we have in mind when we refer to a government agency, a credit union, or a Buddhist ethical culture. We are also forced to recognize, however, that there is enormous and important variation across the instances of these kinds of social formations. Social concepts do not identify social kinds—groups of entities that share fundamentally similar causal and structural constitutions. Third, there is a great deal of path dependence and circumstance in the development of various instances of social entities, depending on the interactions of actors within the course of their development as well as other arbitrary causal factors. Social entities are *contingent* in their composition and properties. Finland, Iceland, and New Zealand have unicameral legislatures, while France, Great Britain, and Germany have bicameral legislatures. The differences between the two systems are important but not systemic; the best explanation of the different forms is simply the different histories of institution-formation the various states underwent. We can summarize these points by observing that social entities are plastic, heterogeneous, and contingent. These ontological characteristics have very important consequences for our understanding of how the social world works.

Consider the feature of plasticity. Virtually all social entities are *plastic* in the sense that they are susceptible to significant change over time, as a result of the purposive and unintentional behavior of the socially constructed individuals who make them up. Organizations, labor unions, universities, churches, and social identities all show a substantial degree of flexibility and fluidity over time, and this fact leads to a substantial degree of heterogeneity among groups of similar social organizations and institutions. This points to a general and important observation about the constitution of the social world: The properties of a social entity or practice can change over time; they are not rigid, fixed, or timeless. They are not bound into consistent and unchanging categories of entities, such as "bureaucratic state," "Islamic society," or "leftist labor organization." Molecules of water preserve their physical characteristics no matter what. But in contrast to natural substances such as gold or water, social things can change their properties indefinitely.

These features of institutional and organizational change are a familiar part of everyday life. Department stores change owners, so the local Marshall Fields becomes a Macy's. More fundamentally, shopping patterns change and Main Street department stores close for good in favor of suburban shopping malls. And in the end online shopping and convenient home delivery systems eventually replace them all. The plasticity of institutions also emerges clearly when we consider longterm economic development. Charles Sabel and Jonathan Zeitlin, for example, demonstrates that firms are strategic and adaptive as they deal with a current set of business challenges (1997). Rather than an inevitable logic of new technologies and their organizational needs, we see a highly adaptive and selective process in which firms pick and choose among alternatives, often mixing the choices to hedge against failure. Sabel and Zeitlin argue that economic actors consider carefully a range of possible changes on the horizon, a set of possible strategic adaptations that might be selected; and they frequently hedge their bets by investing in both the old and the new technology. "Economic agents, we found again and again in the course of the seminar's work, do not maximize so much as they strategize" (1997: 5).

This means that the study of institutional change is very important. James Mahoney and Kathleen Thelen take up this question in *Explaining Institutional Change* (2010). They categorize gradual change into several kinds of processes—displacement, layering, drift, and conversion (2010: 15). And they argue that these kinds of change are significantly different given the different roles that actors and strategies play in each of them. They analyze different types of change in terms of different kinds of social actors, and attribute different kinds of strategies to the different categories of change agents. The theoretical framework Mahoney and Thelen describe is clearly actor-centered. They are focused on identifying the ways in which different categories of actors are empowered to interact with various features of a set of institutional rules. This picture seems to correspond to the ascending and descending links of the macro-micro analysis proposed by Coleman's boat.

These features of stability and change, continuity and discontinuity, in the realm of social institutions correspond very well to the actor-centered view of social entities. To understand structures, organizations, and institutions we need to consider them as the effects of social actors pursuing their plans. States, property systems, constitutions, religious institutions— all these persisting social frames are themselves subject to strategic interventions by the actors who inhabit them, and their properties change over time.

If we adopt this point of view, then the relevant opposition is not between abiding structure and changing circumstance, but rather between long-duration change and short-duration change. What we have is differing degrees of rigidity and different tempos of change attaching to different social structures. And the work by institutional sociologists like Thelen and Pierson is specifically aimed at discovering the forces that lead to the stabilization of an institution or organization—for a while.

Zygmunt Bauman takes a similar view in his idea of "liquid modernity" (2012). This view emphasizes the fact of change within society; and it argues that change is occurring more and more rapidly in the "modern" world. "Forms of modern life may differ in quite a few respects – but what unites them all is precisely their fragility, temporariness, vulnerability and inclination to constant change" (2012: foreword).

Turn now to the feature of heterogeneity that is such an important feature of the social world. A *heterogeneous* group of things is one in which there is a great deal of variation in properties and structure across the members of the group. The basic claim about the heterogeneity of the social comes down to this: at many levels of scale we continue to find a diversity of social things and processes at work. This feature of the social world is related to the point just made about social plasticity. As changes accumulate, slowly or rapidly, social structures, institutions, and organizations show a tendency to diverge from their cousins. There are social mechanisms that may serve to slow down these processes of differentiation—deliberate efforts to maintain organizational features that represent the most effective way of accomplishing a given range of goals, for example—but in general we can expect a broad range of heterogeneity across seemingly similar social entities.

Heterogeneity makes a difference because one of the central goals of positivist science is to discover strong regularities among classes of phenomena, and regularities appear to presuppose homogeneity of the things over which the regularities are thought to obtain. So to observe that social phenomena are deeply heterogeneous at many levels of scale, is to cast fundamental doubt on the goal of discovering strong social regularities.

Let's consider some of the forms of heterogeneity that the social world illustrates. First is the heterogeneity that can be discovered within social categories of things—cities, religions, electoral democracies, social movements. Think of the diversity within Islam documented so well by Clifford Geertz (1968); the diversity at multiple levels that exists among great cities like Beijing, New York, Geneva, and Rio (institutions, demography, ethnic groups, economic characteristics, administrative roles, …); the institutional variety that exists in the electoral democracies of India, France, and Argentina; or the diversity across the social movements of the right. No single specification will suffice to capture all the members of any of these groups of social formations.

Second is the heterogeneity of social causes and influences. Social events are commonly the result of a variety of different kinds of causes that come together in highly contingent conjunctions. A revolution may be caused by a protracted drought, a harsh system of land tenure, a new ideology of peasant solidarity, a communications system that conveys messages to the rural poor, and an unexpected spar within the rulers—all coming together at a moment in time. And this range of causal factors, in turn, shows up in the background of a very heterogeneous set of effects. (A transportation network, for example, may play a causal role in the occurrence of an epidemic, the spread of radical ideas, and a long, slow process of urban settlement.) The causes of an event are a mixed group of dissimilar influences with different dynamics and temporalities, and the effects of a given causal factor are also a mixed and dissimilar group.

Third is the heterogeneity that can be discovered across and within social groups. It is not the case that all Kansans think alike—and this is true for whatever descriptors we might choose in order to achieve greater homogeneity (evangelical Kansans, urban evangelical Kansans, ...). There are always interesting gradients within any social group. Likewise, there is great variation in the nature of ordinary, lived experience—for middle-class French families celebrating *quatorze Juillet*, for Californians celebrating July 4, and for Brazilians enjoying *Dia da Independência* on September 7.

A fourth form of heterogeneity takes us within the agent herself, when we note the variety of motives, moral frameworks, emotions, and modes of agency on the basis of which people act. This is one of the weaknesses of doctrinaire rational choice theory or dogmatic Marxism, the analytical assumption of a single dimension of motivation and reasoning. Instead, it is visible that one person acts for a variety of motives at a given time, persons shift their motives over time, and members of groups differ in terms of their motivational structure as well. So there is heterogeneity of motives and agency within the agent. (This is part of the importance of the theory of intersectionality as a theory of political behavior; Berger and Guidroz 2009.)

These dimensions of heterogeneity make a crucial point: the social world is an ensemble, a dynamic mixture, and an ongoing interaction of forces, agents, structures, and mentalities. Social outcomes emerge from this heterogeneous and dynamic mixture, and the quest for general laws of social change or social uniformity is deeply quixotic.

Where does the heterogeneity principle take us? It suggests an explanatory strategy: instead of looking for laws of whole categories of events and things, rather than searching for simple answers to questions like "why do revolutions occur?", we might instead look to a "concatenation" strategy. That is, we might simply acknowledge the fact of molar heterogeneity and look instead for some of the different processes and things in play in a given item of interest, and the build up a theory of the whole as a concatenation of the particulars of the parts.

Implications for Social Science

Social entities and processes at every level are the contingent and interactive result of the activities of individual actors. Individuals are influenced by the social environment in which they live; so there is no reductionist strategy available here, reducing social properties to purely individual properties. But the key words here are "contingency" and "interactive". There is no systemic or necessary answer to the question, why did Chicago become the metropolis of the central North American continent rather than St. Louis (Cronon 1991)? Instead, there is history—the choices made by early railroad investors and route designers, the availability of timber in Michigan but not Missouri, a particularly effective group of early city politicians in Chicago compared to St. Louis, the comparative influence on the national scene of Illinois and Missouri. These are all contingent and path-dependent factors deriving from the situated choices of actors at various levels of decision making throughout the century. Further, when we push down into lower levels of the filigree of social activity, we find equally contingent processes. Why did Motown come to dominate musical culture for a few decades in Detroit and beyond? Why did professional football take off in the United States but professional soccer did not? Why are dating patterns different in Silicon Valley than Iowa City? None of these questions have law-driven answers. Instead, in every case the answer will be a matter of pathway-tracing, examining the contingent turning points that brought us to the situation in question.

What this argument is meant to make clear is that the social world is not like the natural world. It is fundamentally "historical" (meaning that the present is unavoidably influenced by the past); contingent (meaning that events could have turned out differently); and causally plural (meaning that there is no core set of "social forces" that jointly serve to drive all social change). It also means that there is no "canonical" description of the social world. With classical physics we had the idea that nature could be described as a set of objects with mass and momentum; electromagnetic radiation with properties of frequency and velocity; atoms and molecules with fixed properties and forces; etc. But this is not the case with the social world. New kinds of processes come and go, and it is always open to a social researcher to identify a new trend or process and to attempt to make sense of this process in its context.

This point does not imply that social phenomena do not admit of explanation at all. We can provide mid-level explanations of a vast range of social patterns and events, from the denuding of Michigan forests in the 1900s to the incidence of first names over time. What we cannot do is to provide a general theory that suffices as an explanatory basis for identifying and explaining all social phenomena. The social sciences are at their best when they succeed in identifying mechanisms that underlie familiar social patterns. And these mechanisms are most credible when they are actor-centered, in the sense that they illuminate the ways that individual actors' behavior is influenced or generated so as to produce the outcome in question.

In short: the social realm is ontologically different from the natural realm, and it is crucial for social scientists to have this in mind as they formulate their research and theoretical ideas. This insight, in turn, is very important when we seek to understand the ontology of government, the ways in which government acts through organizational and symbolic means.

REFERENCES

Archer, Margaret Scotford. *Realist Social Theory: The Morphogenetic Approach.* Cambridge and New York: Cambridge University Press, 1995.

Bauman, Zygmunt. *Liquid Modernity.* 2nd ed. Cambridge, UK; Malden, MA: Polity Press; Blackwell, 2012.

Berger, Michele, and Kathleen Guidroz, eds. *The Intersectional Approach Transforming the Academy Through Race, Class, and Gender.* Chapel Hill: University of North Carolina Press, 2009.

Bhaskar, Roy. *Dialectic: The Pulse of Freedom.* London; New York: Verso, 1993.

Boyd, Richard. "Materialism Without Reductionism: What Physicalism Does Not Entail." In *Readings in the Philosophy of Psychology Vol. 1*, edited by Ned Block. Cambridge, MA: Harvard University Press, 1980.

Coleman, James S. *Foundations of Social Theory.* Cambridge: Harvard University Press, 1990.

Cronon, William. *Nature's Metropolis: Chicago and the Great West.* New York: W. W. Norton, 1991.

Elder-Vass, David. *The Causal Power of Social Structures: Emergence, Structure and Agency.* Cambridge: Cambridge University Press, 2010.

Epstein, Joshua. *Generative Social Science: Studies in Agent-Based Computational Modeling*. Princeton, NJ: Princeton University Press, 2006.
Fodor, Jerry. "Special Sciences and the Disunity of Science as a Working Hypothesis." *Synthese* 28, no. 2 (1974): 97–115.
Geertz, Clifford. *Islam Observed; Religious Development in Morocco and Indonesia*. New Haven: Yale University Press, 1968.
Gibbard, Allan. *Wise Choices, Apt Feelings: A Theory of Normative Judgment*. Cambridge: Harvard University Press, 1990.
Granovetter, Mark. "Economic Action and Social Structure: The Problem of Embeddedness." *American Journal of Sociology* 91, no. 3 (1985): 481–510.
Kim, Jaegwon. *Supervenience and Mind: Selected Philosophical Essays*. Cambridge: Cambridge University Press, 1993.
Little, Daniel. *Microfoundations, Method and Causation: On the Philosophy of the Social Sciences*. New Brunswick, NJ: Transaction Publishers, 1998.
Little, Daniel. *New Directions in the Philosophy of Social Science*. London: Rowman & Littlefield Publishers, 2016.
Little, Daniel. "Microfoundations." In *The Routledge Companion to Philosophy of Social Science*, edited by Lee McIntyre and Alex Rosenberg. London; New York: Routledge, 2017.
Luhmann, Niklas, Dirk Baecker, and Peter Gilgen. *Introduction to Systems Theory*. Cambridge, UK; Malden, MA: Polity, 2013.
Mahoney, James, and Kathleen Ann Thelen. *Explaining Institutional Change: Ambiguity, Agency, and Power*. Cambridge; New York: Cambridge University Press, 2010.
Miller, John H., and Scott E. Page. *Complex Adaptive Systems: An Introduction to Computational Models of Social Life*. Princeton: Princeton University Press, 2007.
Morçöl, Göktuğ. *A Complexity Theory for Public Policy*. London: Routledge, 2012.
Sabel, Charles F., and Jonathan Zeitlin. *Worlds of Possibility: Flexibility and Mass Production in Western Industrialization*. Cambridge, UK; New York: Maison des sciences de l'homme: Cambridge University Press, 1997.
Simon, Herbert. "The Architecture of Complexity." *Proceedings of the American Philosophical Society* 106, no. 6 (1962): 467–82.
Wimsatt, William C. "Reductionism and Its Heuristics: Making Methodological Reductionism Honest." *Synthese*, 2006.

CHAPTER 4

Intellectual Tools for Understanding Government

Abstract This chapter introduces a handful of innovative ontological ideas about the social world: strategic action fields, *assemblages* theory, economic and class interests, and recent innovations in organizational sociology. These ideas proceed largely from the actor-centered perspective described in Chapter 1. Recent organizational theories have given additional emphasis to the topic of organizational culture. The theory of strategic action fields holds that organizations are configured around incumbents who are assigned roles and powers that give them both an interest and an ability to maintain the workings of the organization. Power and collaboration play key roles in their construction. The key idea within *assemblages* theory is that there does not exist a fixed and stable ontology of entities for the social world that proceeds from "atoms" to "molecules" to "materials". Rather, social formations are contingent *assemblages* of other complex configurations, and they in turn play roles in other, more extended configurations.

Keywords *Assemblages* theory · Class conflict · Material interest · Organizational sociology · Strategic action fields

In this chapter I introduce a handful of innovative and substantive ideas about how to think about the social world that appear to have a great deal of relevance for understanding the world of government and public administration. These ideas proceed largely from the actor-centered perspective described in Chapter 1, and they provide several different ways of thinking about the basic institutions, structures, and actions of government. Together they contribute to a social ontology of government.

ORGANIZATIONAL SOCIOLOGY

Governments consist of multiple organizations, at a wide range of scales and complexity. Key to understanding the "ontology of government" therefore is the empirical and theoretical challenge of understanding how organizations work. The activities of government encompass organizations across a wide range of scales, from the local office of the Department of Motor Vehicles (forty employees) to the Department of Defense (861,000 civilian employees). Having the best understanding possible of how organizations work and fail is crucial to understanding the workings of government.

Organizational theory as a field has made a great deal of progress in the past two decades. Richard Scott's book *Institutions and Organizations: Ideas, Interests, and Identities* set the stage for much contemporary thinking in the field of organizational studies in the past two decades (Scott 1995). Scott looks at organizations as a particular kind of institution, with differentiating characteristics but commonalities as well. He formulates a series of crucial questions about organizations—questions for which we need answers if we want to know how organizations work, what confers stability upon them, and why and how they change. Out of a long list of questions, several are particularly important for our purposes here: "How are we to regard behavior in organizational settings? Does it reflect the pursuit of rational interests and the exercise of conscious choice, or is it primarily shaped by conventions, routines, and habits?" "Why do individuals and organizations conform to institutions? Is it because they are rewarded for doing so, because they believe they are morally obligated to obey, or because they can conceive of no other way of behaving?" "Why is the behavior of organizational participants often observed to depart from the formal rules and stated goals of the organization?" "Do control systems function only when they are associated with incentives ... or are other processes sometimes at work?" "How do differences in cultural beliefs shape the nature and operation of organizations?" (Introduction).

These are key questions, and a great deal of new research has transpired in the field of organizational studies in attempts to answer them. Another important contribution is Scott and Davis, *Organizations and Organizing: Rational, Natural and Open System Perspectives* (2007). Their book expresses some of the shifts that have taken place in the field since the work of March, Simon, and Perrow (March and Simon 1958; Simon 1997 [1947]; Perrow 2014 [1972]). The word "organizing" in the title signals the idea that organizations are no longer viewed as static structures within which actors carry out well-defined roles; but are instead dynamic processes in which active efforts by leaders, managers, and employees define goals and strategies and work to carry them out. And the "open system" phrase highlights the point that organizations always exist and function within a broader environment—political constraints, economic forces, public opinion, technological innovation, other organizations, and today climate change and environmental disaster.

Scott and Davis emphasize several key ontological elements that any theory of organizations needs to address: the environment in which an organization functions; the strategy and goals of the organization and its powerful actors; the features of work and technology chosen by the organization; the features of formal organization that have been codified (human resources, job design, organizational structure); the elements of "informal organization" that exist in the entity (culture, social networks); and the people of the organization.

They describe three theoretical frameworks through which organizational theories have attempted to approach the empirical analysis of organizations. Each of these frameworks sheds light on the workings of the organizations that make up government. (a) The "rational" framework emphasizes the goal-directedness built into an organization by its founders and custodians, and understands organizational behavior of the participants as rational efforts to accomplish these organizational goals. "From the rational system perspective, organizations are instruments designed to attain specified goals" (45). (b) The "natural systems" framework emphasizes the fact that organizations are contingent assemblages of multiple priorities and motivations, almost always embodying competition over priorities and the allocation of resources. "Organizations are collectivities whose participants are pursuing multiple interests, both disparate and common, but who recognize the value of perpetuating the organization as an important resource. The natural system view emphasizes the common attributes that organizations share with all social collectivities" (39). (c) Finally, the "open-system" framework emphasizes the point that organizations always function within a broader environment of opportunity, meaning, and constraint, and that we cannot understand organizational behavior and structure without paying attention to these broader features of the environment in which the organization exists. "From the open system perspective, environments shape, support, and infiltrate organizations. Connections with 'external' elements can be more critical than those among 'internal' components; indeed, for many functions the distinction between organization and environment is revealed to be shifting, ambiguous, and arbitrary.... Organizations are congeries of interdependent flows and activities linking shifting coalitions of participants embedded in wider material-resource and institutional environments" (40).

The "natural systems" approach described by Scott and Davis is most useful for our reflections about the ontology of government. This approach emphasizes the fact that any organization involves multiple actors with different sets of priorities and purposes, and that individual decision-making within organizations involves culture, norms, and bounded rationality as well as more traditional models of rational purposive behavior. The label "natural systems" is not particularly well chosen, since there is nothing "natural" about an organization. A better phrase is that used by Fligstein and McAdam, the *strategic action fields* approach to the study of organizations (Fligstein and McAdam 2012), or that used by Crozier and Friedberg, the *actor-system* approach (Crozier and Friedberg 1980). However, the label is now entrenched within the literature of contemporary organization theory, so I will use it here as well.

A crucial question for organizational theory concerns the way that theorists think about the actors within organizations. Both the natural and the open-systems frameworks reject the simplifying assumption that organizational actors are fully guided by the organization's priorities, processes, and rules. Instead, organizational theorists have come to pay more attention to the non-rational components of organizational behavior—values, cultural affinities, cognitive frameworks and expectations. This approach does not eliminate the idea that organizations are purposive and actors are rational, but it broadens the scope of our understanding of both poles of the question.

Elinor Ostrom's writings on what she calls "common-property resource regimes" are relevant in this context as well. She focuses on the informal organizations, practices, and non-market institutions that human communities have created as solutions to environmental and resource-depletion challenges (Ostrom 1990). Like the approach taken in this book, Ostrom too proceeds from a "situated actor" perspective in her attempt at analyzing complex institutional situations, placing the "action situation" at the center of her analysis, and she analyzes collective behavior within a complex ecological setting involving resource systems, ambient institutions, and concrete social relationships. McGinnis and Ostrom (2014) describe this approach as a "social-ecological system" framework; and it shares a number of assumptions with the open-system framework described here within organizational studies.

This emphasis on finding a broader perspective on organizations leads to an important shift of emphasis in next-generation ideas about organizations, involving an emphasis on informal practices, norms, and behaviors that exist within organizations. Rather than looking at an organization as a rational structure implementing mission and strategy, contemporary organization theory confirms the idea that informal practices, norms, and cultural expectations are ineliminable parts of organizational behavior. The idea of organizational culture has come to play a more prominent role in organizational studies. "*Culture* describes the pattern of values, beliefs, and expectations more or less shared by the organization's members.... These components hang together as a more-or-less coherent theory that guides the organization's more formalized policies and strategies" (Scott and Davis 2007: 33). Contemporary organizational theory pays substantial attention to the micro-cultures that are operative in various organizations.

The work of Scott and Davis in organizational theory is of particular interest here because it supports analysis of the key issue defining this book: how does government work, and what ontological assumptions do we need to make in order to better understand the successes and failures of government action? The key topic of organizational dysfunction finds a very comfortable home in the theoretical spaces created by the intellectual frameworks of organizational studies described by Scott and Davis.

Strategic Action Fields

Neil Fligstein and Doug McAdam offer an important example of the natural and open-systems approaches described above in their theory of strategic action fields (Fligstein and McAdam 2012). The basic idea is that the fundamental structure of social life is "agents behaving strategically within a field of resources and other agents," and that this perspective is as relevant in organizations and firms as it is in social movements. Here is their preliminary description of the idea of a strategic action field. "A strategic action field is a constructed mesolevel social order in which actors (who can be individual or collective) are attuned to and interact with one another on the basis of shared (which is not to say consensual) understandings about the purposes of the field, relationships to others in the field (including who has power and why), and the rules governing legitimate action in the field. A stable field is one in which the main actors are able to reproduce themselves and the field over a fairly long period of time" (Fligstein and McAdam 2012: 1).

Fligstein and McAdam do not give *fundamental* ontological status to structures or organizations. Instead, organizations are ensembles of agents-in-fields, at a range of levels. Organizations are configured around incumbents who are assigned roles and powers that give them both an interest and an ability to maintain the workings of the organization. They put it forward that "strategic action fields ... are the fundamental units of collective action in society" (Fligstein and McAdam 2011: 3). Power and advantage play key roles in their construction: "We too see SAFs as socially constructed arenas within which actors with varying resource endowments vie for advantage. Membership in these fields is based far more on subjective 'standing' than objective criteria" (3).

Crucially for our purposes, they extend this framework to formal organizations such as business firms and government agencies. "Firms are nested strategic action fields in which there are hierarchical dependent relationships between the component fields. Each plant and office is a strategic action field in its own right. Typically firms are organized into larger divisions in which management controls resource allocation and hiring" (Fligstein and McAdam 2012: 59). So stability and continuity are not primitive characteristics of an organization; instead, stability is a consequence of the specific interlocking assignments of interests and powers within the various networks of agents that make up the organization. Stability is a dynamic feature of the organization, reproduced by the actions of incumbents. And change in the organization occurs when there is significant alteration in those interests and powers.

How do our concepts of meso-level social structures like institutions and organizations change when we use the language of strategic action fields? And substantively, how can we account for the relative level of stability that organizations and institutions possess, if they are simply composites of strategically motivated actors? This description suggests a high degree of fluidity, as strategies and coalitions shift. But instead, we observe a high level of stability in organizations much of the time, persisting over multiple generations of actors. The answer derives from the idea that Fligstein and McAdam introduce of "internal governance units": "In addition to incumbents and challengers, many strategic action fields have internal governance units that are charged with overseeing compliance with field rules and, in general, facilitating the overall smooth functioning and reproduction of the system" (Fligstein and McAdam 2012: 13). On this approach, then, stability is a consequence of the configuration of a given system of strategic fields, rather than an axiomatic property of the organization.

There are several features of this approach that are valuable for our purposes here. One is the fact that it directly challenges the tendency towards reification that sometimes blocks sociological thinking—the idea that social "things" like states persist largely independently from the individuals who make them up. The strategic-fields approach leads to a way of thinking about the social world that emphasizes contingency and plasticity rather than rigid and homogeneous social structures. Second, the approach encourages us to look inside the organization to try to identify the networks of authority, influence, and coordination through which the activities of the organization transpire. This approach is valuable when it comes to considering the workings of government agencies.

Assemblage Theory

Let us turn now to a very different ontological idea, the conception of society as an "assemblage" of multiple different kinds of social configurations. Gilles Deleuze and Félix Guattari's (1987) theory of *assemblage* as a way of thinking about the social world is an intriguing one. Fundamentally the idea is that there does not exist a fixed and stable ontology of entities for the social world that proceeds from "atoms" to "molecules" to "materials". Rather, social formations are assemblages of other complex configurations, and they in turn play roles in other, more extended configurations.

Manuel DeLanda (2006) provides an account of assemblage theory that is directly relevant to research in the human and social sciences.

DeLanda explicates "assemblage" by saying what it is not. First, assemblage theory is opposed to essentialism and reification (26 ff.). DeLanda emphasizes that Deleuze's concept resists the "organismic" approach to conceptualizing the social, by which he means an approach that looks at the whole as an inextricable combination of interrelated parts. This implies that the parts are implicated in each other; the organismic perspective emphasizes the internal connectedness of a thing. DeLanda distinguishes between "interiority" and "exteriority" in conceptualizing the components of a thing. For assemblage theory, the relations among the parts are contingent, not necessary. And, crucially, according to assemblage theory, parts can be extracted from one whole and inserted into another. "These relations imply, first of all, that a component part of an assemblage may be detached from it and plugged into a different assemblage in which its interactions are different. In other words, the exteriority of relations implies a certain autonomy for the terms they relate" (10–11). "Interior" relations among things are essential, logical, or semantic; whereas exterior relations are contingent and non-essential. Identifying a pair as husband and wife is to identify an interior relation; identifying a pair as a female architect and a male nightclub bouncer is an exterior relation. Another aspect of the theory, according to DeLanda, is the fact that it does not privilege one level of organization over another. "Micro" is not more fundamental than "macro"; instead, social reality is "multiscaled" (38), with assemblages occurring at every level.

What does this mean in practical terms? As a first approximation, the core idea of *assemblage* is that social things (cities, structures, ideologies) are composed of an overlapping and contingent collection of a heterogeneous set of social activities and practices. The relations among these activities and practices are contingent, and the properties of the composite thing—the assemblage—are likewise a contingent and "emergent" sum of the properties of the component threads. The composite has no "essence"—just a contingent and changeable set of properties. A simplified expression of assemblage theory might consist of the following ideas:

1. Social entities are composed of components and lesser systems.
2. The components of a social entity are heterogeneous.
3. The components include both material factors and meaningful expressions.
4. The components have their own characteristics and dynamics.

4 INTELLECTUAL TOOLS FOR UNDERSTANDING GOVERNMENT   61

5. The components may have very different temporal and spatial scales.
6. The effects and interactions among components may be indeterminate because of complexity effects and probabilistic causal mechanisms.
7. The behavior of the whole is difficult or impossible to calculate even given extensive knowledge of the dynamics of the components.

This formulation suggests that large social entities are "messy" but still amenable to analysis and study; and this is what sociology requires. Moreover, this approach encourages social scientists to arrive at partial explanations of social features by discerning the dynamics of some of the components. These accounts are necessarily incomplete, because they ignore many other constituents of the assembled whole. And yet they are potentially explanatory, when the dynamics being studied have the ability to generate trans-assemblage characteristics (continuity, crisis).

What is appealing about this way of thinking about the social world is that it takes us away from the presuppositions we often bring about the social world as consisting of a range of discrete social objects or things. According to this static way of thinking, the state is a thing with fixed properties composed of other things; likewise Islam is an extended social thing; likewise Chicago; and so on. The assemblage approach suggests a different set of metaphors for the social world: mosaic, patchwork, heterogeneity, fluidity, transitory configuration. This appears to be a more insightful way of characterizing large extended social formation like states or regulatory agencies.

An important virtue of the treatment here is that DeLanda makes a strong case for a social ontology that is both anti-reductionist and anti-essentialist. Social things have properties that we do not need to attempt to reduce to properties of ensembles of components; but social things are not transcendent, essential wholes whose behavior is independent from the activities of the individuals and lower-level configurations of which they consist. Further, this view of social ontology has an important implication that DeLanda explicitly calls out: we need to recognize the fact of downward causation from social configurations (individual assemblages) to the actions of the individuals and lesser configurations of which they consist. A community embodying a set of norms about deference and respectful behavior in fact elicits these forms of behavior in the individuals who make up the community. This is so through the very ordinary fact that individuals monitor each others' behavior and sometimes retaliate when norms are breached.

Economic Interests and Influence

We cannot understand government without bringing forward the fact of economic interests and influence stemming from the broader distribution of property rights in the society within which government exists. Karl Marx had something of a theory of politics and somewhat less than a theory of government. (Ralph Miliband makes much the same point about Marx's limitations as a political scientist; Miliband 1965.) The slogan "the capitalist state serves as the managing committee of the bourgeoisie" represents the simplest version of his view of the state. Marx generally regarded government and law as an expression of class interests.

That said, Marx was not much of an organizational thinker. He had virtually nothing to say about the workings of real governments—the British state or the French state, for example, and nothing to say about the ministries and bureaus through which the affairs of government worked. When he mentioned politicians in any European country it was as particular individuals rather than as functionaries. And yet it is crucial to understand government—including nineteenth-century European governments—as bureaucracies organizing the flows of revenue, regulations, information, and coercion. Marx added little to this task.

Most of Marx's ideas about the state and government were formulated during the years surrounding the revolutions of 1848, including especially the *Communist Manifesto* and *The Eighteenth Brumaire of Louis Bonaparte* (Marx 1974; Marx and Engels 1974). The view that Marx expresses there is unambiguous. He describes the state within capitalism as the naked expression of the economic interests of the bourgeoisie, imposed on the whole of society through control of the state.

This is a particularly reductionist interpretation of politics, but it has important ontological implications. It highlights a strong relationship between class interests and the actions of the state. Politicians are the creatures of various propertied interests, and their actions are dictated by their patrons. But towards the end of the *Eighteenth Brumaire* Marx gives a nod to the complexity and size of government. This clearly presents a valuable topic for study: how does this "machinery of government" work? What is the social ontology of the ministries, offices, and agencies of government? Further, Marx raises a point that Nicos Poulantzas eventually characterizes as the "relative autonomy of the capitalist state" (1973).

Marx might have defended his relative neglect of the workings of government on the ground that the existence and functioning of bureaucracy in government are second-order factors, and that the main question is the existence and use of political power through the tools of state action. How precisely this is implemented was not of scientific interest to Marx, and he believed he had a more fundamental understanding of the orientation and workings of government. This is his view that political power derives from class privilege and that state organs act in support of class interests. Further, we can easily see some of the mechanisms through which actors with substantial economic interests (large property, corporations, landowners, owners of railroads and other key infrastructure) are in positions to influence or determine the actions of government and its agencies: financial support and inducements for legislators, the quiet power associated with the ability to pay for experts and lobbyists to make the case for favorable legislation and rule-writing, and the background threat of "capital strike"—a regime that is excessively restrictive of propertied interests may witness the flight of capital and jobs to more favorable jurisdictions (Domhoff 1970; Miliband 1969). Culpepper (2010) explores the mechanisms of quiet politics exercised by propertied interests in four leading capitalist democracies.)

What can we take away from Marx's writings that is pertinent to the current subject, the ontology of the state? There appear to be several valuable ideas. First is the fact of the intertwining of large economic interests with the structure and actions of the state. Whether we think of the French or English states of the nineteenth century, or of the modern US state, it is plain that economic power has major implications for political power and state action. Corporations have the ability to shape policy through their lobbying efforts and an ideology that "what is good for General Motors is good for the United States"—that is, a supposed but fictional identity of interest between corporate property and the whole of society. Economic power and political ideology influence the state and its administration, and it is valuable to undertake to trace out some of those lines of influence.

Second is the germ of the idea of "relative state autonomy" from economic interests—Marx's idea that state institutions acquire a kind of stability to some extent that permits state agencies and executives to sometimes take actions that are not preferred by the propertied classes. This idea lays open the intellectual possibilities of the field of institutionalist analysis of public administration. The first idea creates the intellectual space for sociologists and political scientists such as C. Wright Mills (1956), Ralph Miliband (1969), Charles Perrow (2002), and William Domhoff (1970) to study the concrete avenues through which corporate and economic power influence state action. The second creates the opportunity to study more carefully the institutions of government, bureaucracy, and administration, and discover through a better understanding of their concrete workings how the "relative autonomy" permits the emergence of states as diverse as Thatcher and Reagan's conservative pro-business regimes and the sometimes-successful social democracies of western and northern Europe countries—the Nordic model. Esping-Andersen's work is useful here (1985).

Finally, we can take seriously the suggestion that Marx appears to make that the orienting effects of economic power are sufficiently pervasive and deep that "determination in the last instance" makes permanent state policy favoring workers' interests over large private-property interests unlikely.

POWER

It is perhaps trivial to say that governments reflect and wield power, and that "power" must be counted among the components of any adequate ontology of government. But what is power, as a social entity or condition? Does "power" exist, or is it a term that encompasses a range of other social things and relations? Here are a few visible features of power. Power is the ability held by one individual or group to influence or coerce the behavior of another individual or group. Power derives from the individual's or group's position within the structure of society in terms of which the power-holder is able to gather resources for influencing the behavior of others. Power is created by access to social and material resources that permit an individual or group to control or influence social outcomes, including the behavior of other individuals and groups, the distribution of things, and the configuration of social institutions. Those levers might include relations with conformant legislators positioned to enact legislation and regulation, command of military or police forces, relations with conformant private citizens positioned to coerce their dependents to behave this way or that, or access to economically influential private

4 INTELLECTUAL TOOLS FOR UNDERSTANDING GOVERNMENT 65

actors who can use their economic position to compel compliance from others..

Michael Mann's important theoretical and historical analysis of social power identifies four primary sources of social power: ideological, economic, military, and political (Mann 1986). Mann's work serves to broaden the concept of power by grouping the levers of coercion into different families: economic coercion, physical coercion, political power, and ideological power. This allows us to identify the sources of power within a given society. Individuals and groups who are favorably positioned with respect to these different categories of instruments of coercion are more powerful than others.

On this approach, "power" is a characteristic attaching to individuals and groups who are in a position to invoke access to certain kinds of instruments of coercion. What is "coercion"? We might define coercion very simply in terms of an actor's ability to influence the terms of choice that confront another actor. Here is a possible definition: x coerces y to perform O when x creates a choice situation for y in which the costs of choosing other available options are unacceptably high, leaving only O to be chosen. We can then broaden this concept to groups in society by postulating that certain groups have greater access to the levers of coercion than others. So we might say that "owners of property have more power than workers" because owners have access to the lever of unemployment, whereas workers have access only to the power to withhold their labor at substantial personal and familial cost. And we might say that organized crime lords have more power than shopkeepers because the criminals have greater ability to use and threaten violence against the shopkeeper than the reverse.

What this account leaves out is the range of "soft" power associated with framing and ideology. This is a different avenue of social influence. It is possible to impel individuals or groups towards certain kinds of actions by shaping their beliefs and cognitive-affective frameworks. Using the media to shift the terms of debate over a policy—creating a rhetoric of "death panels" to encourage opposition to universal health insurance—is a way of exerting power without coercion.

A few features of "power" emerge from these simple descriptions. First, power is a relational concept. An individual possesses power over other individuals (relation 1) and does so in virtue of the relations he or she bears to other persons and institutions (relation 2). Second, power is the activity side of structure: structures and sets of social relations constitute the environment within which individuals are empowered to exercise power over others. The structures persist over time, and individuals act within their elements to exert their will over others.

Steven Lukes's *Power: A Radical View* was a very important contribution when it appeared in 1974 (2005 [1974]). Lukes emphasized several important points that became landmarks in subsequent discussions of the social reality of power: that power is a multi-dimensional social factor, that power and democracy are paradoxically related, and that there are very important non-coercive sources of power in modern society.

Lukes offers a generic definition of power along these lines: "I have defined the concept of power by saying that A exercises power over B when A affects B in a manner contrary to B's interests" (Lukes 2005: 37). But this definition is too generic, and Lukes attempts to provide a more satisfactory interpretation by constructing a "three-dimensional" account of power. He begins his account with the treatment of power provided by the pluralist tradition of American democratic theory, including especially Robert Dahl in "The Concept of Power" (1957). This is the one-dimensional view: power is a behavioral attribute that applies to individuals to the extent that they are able to modify the behavior of other individuals within a decision-making process. The person with the power in a situation is the person who prevails in the decision-making process (Lukes 2005: 18).

The second dimension that Lukes discusses was brought forward in rebuttal to this pluralist theory; critics pointed out that it is possible to influence decisions by shaping the agenda, not merely by weighing in on existing decision points. Lukes quotes from Peter Bachrach and Morton Baratz (1962) in "Two Faces of Power": "to the extent that a person or group – consciously or unconsciously – creates or reinforces barriers to the public airing of policy conflicts, that person or group has power" (20). So shaping the agenda is an important source of power that is overlooked in the pluralist model, the one-dimensional view.

The third dimension of power considered by Lukes is a response to a different problem—the fact that people sometimes act willingly in ways that appear contrary to their most basic interests. So the third dimension is the set of ways in which the powerful transform the powerless in such a way that the latter behave as the former wish without coercion or forcible constraint—for example, by creating a pervasive system of ideology or false consciousness. Both pluralists and their critics overlook an important point, in Lukes's view: these theories of power "... ignore the crucial point that the most effective and insidious use of power is to prevent such conflict from arising in the first place" (Lukes 2005: 27). To make clear his meaning concerning the third dimension of power Lukes shifts his language to refer to "power as domination." Domination can occur through explicit coercive means, but it can also occur through unconscious mechanisms.

We can give a simple schematic description of the chief mechanisms and tactics through which control and influence are exercised in contemporary society: coercion, threat, manipulation of the agenda, manipulation of information and thought, and positional advantage. These are almost all *relational* characteristics—they have to do with the relationships of influence that exist among individuals and groups.

Further, power is distributed over many individuals and groups within society at a time. But it is fluid and subject to fluctuations as structures and individuals change. Mayor Richard Daley was powerful at one point in time but not at other points. And what changed was not Daley but the levers of power and social networks to which he had access as party leader, mayor, and holder of social capital. These points imply that power is a relational characteristic that exists at various social locations depending on the connections those locations have to the levers of influence over individuals and groups. Power can be wielded in multiple ways: direct threat and coercion, manipulation of incentives, manipulation of the agenda to give preference to certain outcomes, and quiet influence and lobbying.

In 1956 C. Wright Mills offered a middle-level sociology of power in America in *The Power Elite* (1956). Mills believed that power in the America of the 1950s centers in the economic, political, and military domains—corporations, the state, and the military are all organized around networks of influence at the top of which stands a relatively small number of extremely powerful people. Mills defines power as the ability to achieve what one wants over the opposition of others; and the levers of power are the great institutions in society—corporations, political institutions, and the military. And the thesis is that a relatively compact group of people exercise close to a monopoly of power in each of these areas. Moreover, power leads often to wealth, in that power permits firms and individuals to gain access to society's wealth. So a power elite is often also an economic elite. Here is a compact description of Mills's conception of the power elite: "The power elite is composed of men whose positions enable them to transcend the ordinary environments of ordinary men and women; they are in positions to make decisions having major consequences. Whether they do or do not make such decisions is less important than the fact that they do occupy such pivotal positions: their failure to act, their failure to make decisions, is itself an act that is often of greater consequence than the decisions they do make. For they are in command of the major hierarchies and organizations of modern society. They rule the big corporations. They run the machinery of the state and claim its prerogatives. They direct the military establishment. They occupy the strategic command posts of the social structure, in which are now centered the effective means of the power and the wealth and the celebrity which they enjoy" (Mills 1956: 73).

Mills' theory can be stated fairly simply. There is a small subset of the American population that (a) possess a number of social characteristics in common (for example, elite university educations, membership in certain civic organizations); (b) are socially interconnected with each other through marriage, friendship, and business relationship; (c) occupy social positions that give them a durable ability to make a large number of the most momentous decisions for American society; (d) are largely insulated from effective oversight from democratic institutions (press, regulatory system, political constraint). They are an elite; they are a socially interconnected group; they possess durable power; and they are little constrained by open and democratic processes.

Is there a power elite today? In one sense it is obvious what the answer is. Corporations continue to have enormous influence on our society—banks, energy companies, pharmaceutical companies, food corporations. In fact, the collective power of corporations in modern societies is surely much greater than it was fifty years ago, through direct economic action and through their ability to influence laws and regulations. Their directors and CEOs do in fact constitute a small and interlocked portion of the population. And these leaders continue to have great ability to determine social outcomes through their "private" decisions about the conduct of the corporation. Moreover, as we will see in a later chapter, there is very little regulative oversight over their decisions and choices. So the existence of a "power elite" is almost a visible fact in today's world. (Scholars like Thomas Dye continue to document the role that small circles of powerful men and women play in economics, politics, and social life in the United States; Dye 2014; Dye et al. 2011.)

REFERENCES

Bachrach, Peter, and Morton S. Baratz. "Two Faces of Power." *American Political Science Review* 56, no. 4 (1962): 947–52.
Crozier, Michel, and Erhard Friedberg. *Actors and Systems: The Politics of Collective Action*. Chicago: University of Chicago Press, 1980.
Culpepper, Pepper. *Quiet Politics and Business Power: Corporate Control in Europe and Japan*. Cambridge ; New York: Cambridge University Press, 2010.
Dahl, Robert A. "The Concept of Power." *Behavioral Science* 2, no. 3 (1957): 201–15.
DeLanda, Manuel. *A New Philosophy of Society: Assemblage Theory and Social Complexity*. London; New York: Continuum International Publishing Group, 2006.
Deleuze, Gilles, and Félix Guattari. *A Thousand Plateaus: Capitalism and Schizophrenia*. Minneapolis: University of Minnesota Press, 1987.
Domhoff, G. William. *The Higher Circles; the Governing Class in America*. 1st ed. New York: Random House, 1970.
Dye, Thomas R. *Who's Running America? The Obama Reign*. 18th ed. London: Routledge, 2014.
Dye, Thomas R., Harmon Zeigler, and Louis Schubert. *The Irony of Democracy: An Uncommon Introduction to American Politics*. 15th ed. Boston: Cengage Learning, 2011.
Esping-Andersen, Gosta. *Politics Against Markets: The Social Democratic Road to Power*. Princeton: Princeton University Press, 1985.
Fligstein, Neil, and Doug McAdam. "Toward a General Theory of Strategic Action Fields." *Sociological Theory* 29, no. 1 (2011): 1–26.
Fligstein, Neil, and Doug McAdam. *A Theory of Fields*. New York: Oxford University Press, 2012.
Lukes, Steven. *Power : A Radical View*. 2nd ed. London; New York: Macmillan, 2005 [1974].
Mann, Michael. *The Sources of Social Power. A History of Power from the Beginning to A.D. 1760*. Vol. 1. Cambridge: Cambridge University Press, 1986.
March, James G., and Herbert A. Simon. *Organizations*. New York: Wiley, 1958.
Marx, Karl. "The Eighteenth Brumaire of Louis Bonaparte." In *Surveys from Exile*, edited by David Fernbach. New York: Vintage, 1974.
Marx, Karl, and Frederick Engels. "The Communist Manifesto." In *The Revolutions of 1848: Political Writings, Vol. I.*, edited by David Fernbach. New York: Vintage, 1974.
McGinnis, Michael D., and Elinor Ostrom. "Social-Ecological System Framework: Initial Changes and Continuing Challenges." *Ecology and Society* 19, no. 2 (2014): art. 30.
Miliband, Ralph. "Marx and the State." *The Socialist Register*, 1965.

Miliband, Ralph. *The State in Capitalist Society*. New York: Basic, 1969.
Mills, C. Wright. *The Power Elite*. New York: Oxford University Press, 1956.
Ostrom, Elinor. *Governing the Commons: The Evolution of Institutions for Collective Action*. Cambridge, UK; New York: Cambridge University Press, 1990.
Perrow, Charles. *Complex Organizations: A Critical Essay*. 3rd ed. Brattleboro, VT: Echo Point Books and Media, 2014 [1972].
Perrow, Charles. *Organizing America: Wealth, Power, and the Origins of Corporate Capitalism*. Princeton, NJ: Princeton University Press, 2002.
Poulantzas, Nicos. *Political Power and Social Class*. London: New Left Books, 1973.
Scott, W. Richard. *Institutions and Organizations*. Thousand Oaks, CA : Sage, 1995.
Scott, W. Richard, and Gerald F. Davis. *Organizations and Organizing: Rational, Natural, and Open System Perspectives*. 1st ed. Upper Saddle River, NJ: Pearson Prentice Hall, 2007.
Simon, Herbert A. *Administrative Behavior: A Study of Decision-Making Processes in Administrative Organizations*. 4th ed. New York: Free Press, 1997 [1947].

CHAPTER 5

Institutions, Norms, and Networks

Abstract Structures, normative systems, and institutions are *things* with sufficient fixity over time and sufficient firmness to permit them to be regarded as social entities. This chapter considers the ontological status of higher-level social entities. Institutions and normative systems are social configurations that have enduring properties that are largely independent of the individuals whom they encompass. They affect the behavior of individuals within them, and they affect the outcomes that individuals achieve through their efforts. Further, they are causally influential in large processes of social change and social stability. Institutions work through the creation of roles, incentives, motivations, and cultural frameworks to coordinate the behavior of participants within their scope. We might define a norm as *a socially embodied* and *individually perceived imperative* that such-and-so an action in a given context must be performed in such-and-so a fashion. The chapter considers some of the aggregative processes that serve as microfoundations for entities like institutions, cultures, and normative systems.

Keywords Corruption · Institutions · New institutionalism · Normative systems · Organizational culture · Social networks

Scientific realism in the social sciences affirms the reality of unobservable social structures, institutions, cultures, and systems of rules and norms. In ordinary thinking, these social configurations have enduring properties that are largely independent of the individuals whom they encompass; they affect the behavior of individuals within them, and they affect the outcomes that individuals achieve through their efforts; and they are causally influential in large processes of social change and social stability. Workers enter a labor market that is largely independent of their own choices and actions. Structures, normative systems, and institutions are *things* with sufficient fixity over time and sufficient firmness to permit them to be regarded as social entities. Likewise, governments are composed of a range of institutions; the actors within governments operate within a variety of normative and cultural frameworks; and actors inside and outside of government fall within a very great range of social networks. All of these facts are both common knowledge and a bit mysterious, and they are critical for the effort of providing a social ontology of government. It is the work of this chapter to provide current thinking in the social sciences to bear on each of these social realities.

Institutions

Institutions are interlocking sets of rules and practices that shape specific sets of actors to behave this way rather than that. Institutions work through the creation of roles, incentives, motivations, and cultural frameworks to coordinate the behavior of participants within their scope. An institution assigns roles to individuals, roles that prescribe their behavior in a range of circumstances. An institution embodies a complex of behavioral rules for those who fall within its scope—a police officer must conform to a specified list of rules for the use of force, a bureaucrat must conform to the rules of conflict of interest of the institution, a college professor must be available to meet with her students in office hours several hours a week. An institution assigns authority and responsibility to various roles and individuals. The chief of police has the authority to enforce discipline among police officers; the department chair has the authority to ensure that professors meet with their classes at the scheduled times. Finally, an institution consists of a complex set of practices and habits. These may be rule-defined, but they may also be informal and unspoken. The practice of members of an office in a business firm contributing to a gift for a departing colleague is not mandated by the rules of the company, but it may be an enduring part of the practice of the company. As the new institutionalism makes very clear, institutions have great resilience and staying power, even as they are subject to internal processes and mechanisms of change.

Institutions are generally thought of as "shaping" factors on human action and choice; individuals construct their actions and strategies within the context of the rules and norms of various institutions. But how do the rules of an organization actually constrain behavior? Mahoney and Thelen (2010) do not take compliance within an institution as a given; instead, they look for the interests and opportunities of various agents within the organization or institution that interlock to secure compliance. This parallels the idea of "governance units" in the Fligstein and McAdam theory of strategic action fields.

A critical ontological question arises when we consider some of these ideas about institutions. This is the requirement of having "microfoundations" at the level of the actors within the institution for the rules, norms, and practices that make up the institution. The need for this kind of analysis is evident from the actor-centered approach to the social world described in Chapter 1; social facts proceed from the circumstances of socially embodied individuals. Enforcing a set of rules is not cost-free; so what is it that allows an institution or organization to maintain its structure of rules of behavior over an extended period of time? Likewise, what facts at the level of the individuals within an institution provide the social reality of the roles of authority and responsibility that exist and that constitute the hierarchies of power and authority within the institution?

Here are some very fundamental questions that we can ask about social institutions. How are institutions formed? How do they work—what are the conformance mechanisms that exist within institutions that induce participants to conform to the rules? What factors support the stability of an institution over time? What kinds of processes lead to change within institutions over time? Why are institutions sometimes swept away and replaced wholesale? What are the microfoundations at the level of various actors and stakeholders through which institutions operate and change? These are among the most fundamental questions that theories of institutions need to answer—how do they start, how are they sustained, and how do they change. And they are unmistakably important in discussing the ontological underpinnings of governments and their actions.

The nature of institutions and their causal properties have received renewed attention through the "new institutionalism" in sociology

(Brinton and Nee 1998; Powell and DiMaggio 1991; Thelen and Conran 2016). This approach is a particularly promising prism through which to understand a great deal of social behavior and change. The new institutionalism is essentially a marriage of the familiar assumptions of applied purposive rationality with the observation that "institutions matter"— that is, that the behavior of purposive individuals depends critically on the institutional constraints within which they act, and the institutional constraints themselves are under-determined by material and economic circumstances. So institutions evolve in response to the strategic actions of a field of actors. The approach stipulates a very tight relationship between institutions and norms regulating behavior. The approach pays close attention to the importance of transaction costs in economic activity (the costs of supervision of a work force, for example, or the cost of collecting information on compliance with a contract). And it postulates that institutions emerge and persist as a solution to specific problems of social coordination.

The new institutionalists have largely focused on the *maintenance and evolution* of major social and political institutions. So Kathleen Thelen's (2004) book, *How Institutions Evolve: The Political Economy of Skills in Germany, Britain, the United States, and Japan*, examines the stability and change within the institutions through which skill is transmitted, Paul Pierson (2004) looks at issues of temporality within institutional change in *Politics in Time: History, Institutions, and Social Analysis*, and Elinor Ostrom (1990) examines institutions through which communities solve common-property resource problems in *Governing the Commons: The Evolution of Institutions for Collective Action*. In each case the analysis begins with the institution already well developed.

Topics of central concern to the practitioners of the new institutionalism include principal-agent problems (the costs of ensuring that one's agents are performing their functions according to the interests of the principal); the design of alternative systems of property rights; collective action problems; and mechanisms of collective decision-making. In each instance the analysis is designed to illuminate the ways in which institutional arrangements have been selected (or have evolved) in such ways as to respond to an important element of transaction costs. It bears pointing out that this approach does not assume that "optimal" institutions emerge, since the actual institutions selected depend on the distribution of political power across groups and their antecedent interests. This point is richly born out in Robert Bates's important arguments concerning government agricultural policies in other parts of Africa (1981) and also in Jack Knight's efforts to frame the conflictual elements of institutions (1992).

An important question of particular contemporary interest within this tradition is how institutions change. Mahoney and Thelen (2010) and Thelen and Conran (2016) address this question directly. The theory they offer of gradual institutional change is an actor-centered theory. Incremental change occurs as the result of the opportunistic and strategic choices made by a range of actors within the institution. In this respect it resembles the theories discussed earlier of Fligstein and McAdam in their theory of strategic action fields.

Other researchers have addressed the workings of institutions by focusing on the ways that institutions shape the actors' behavior. Thornton and Ocasio (2008) define the "institutional logics" perspective "... as the socially constructed, historical patterns of cultural symbols and material practices, including assumptions, values, and beliefs, by which individuals and organizations provide meaning to their daily activity, organize time and space, and reproduce their lives and experiences" (101). They amplify this definition in a later article by identifying four features common to all institutional logics: "sources of collective identity; determinants of power and status; systems of social classification and categorization; and allocation of attention" (Ocasio et al. 2017: 1002). Ocasio et al. (2017) illustrate the linkages postulated by institutional logics by specifying a few mechanisms that do the relevant work: for example, the formation of collective identities, competition for status, social classification (a cognitive mechanism), and salience and attention (Ocasio et al. 2017: 111–114). These are concrete cognitive and social mechanisms through which institutions influence behavior.

The key point here is that institutions often work by shaping by the institution of the actor's cognitive and practical frames. This parallels the idea of that "cognitive/emotional frames" are important in defining the social actor that was highlighted in the discussion in Chapter 4 of new organizational theory. And this makes it a valuable contribution to the richer theory of the actor. The idea is that one's inculcation into a set of religious practices or an occupation produces a distinctive set of attitudes, emotions, beliefs, and processes of reasoning through which individuals perceive and act upon their environment.

The institutional-logics approach is intended to serve both as metatheory and as methodology. It suggests avenues of research for sociologists and it poses questions that require empirical answers. Accordingly, Thornton et al. (2012) illustrate the linkages postulated by institutional logics between level by specifying a few mechanisms that do the relevant work: for example, the formation of collective identities, competition for status, social classification (a cognitive mechanism), and salience and attention. These are reasonably concrete cognitive and social mechanisms through which institutions influence behavior. What is particularly useful about this approach is that it provides a deliberate effort to offer a more nuanced theory of the social actor, it recognizes heterogeneity across institutions and settings, it is deliberately cross-level in its approach, and it focuses on a search for the mechanisms that carry out the forms of influence postulated by the approach.

Normative Systems

Individuals are not "*tabula rasa*" when they interact in social settings. They are not pure rational calculators, seeking to behave so as to bring about the best possible outcomes for themselves. Rather, they are sometimes altruists, caring parents, committed union members, and religious adherents. (It goes without saying that individuals are also purposive and often self-interested.) We can sum up this fact by saying that individuals act out of a combination of normative commitments and purposive, strategic motivation. As Amartya Sen says in "Rational Fools" (1977), "the purely economic man is indeed close to being a social moron" (335). Rather, individuals possess commitments and norms that play a genuine role in their social actions.

We can offer mundane examples of social norms deriving from a wide range of social situations: norms of politeness, norms of fairness, norms of appropriate dress, norms of behavior in business meetings, norms of gendered behavior, and norms of body language and tone of voice in police work. In each case we suppose that (a) there is a publicly recognized norm governing the specified conduct within a specific social group, (b) the norm influences individual behavior in some way, and (c) sanctions and internal motivations come into the explanation of conformant behavior. Norm-breakers may come in for rough treatment by the people around them—which may induce them to honor the norm in the future.

And norm-conformers may do so because they have internalized a set of inhibitions about the proscribed behavior.

We need to have a fairly clear idea of what we mean by a norm. We might define a norm as *a socially embodied* and *individually perceived imperative* that such-and-so an action in a given context must be performed in such-and-so a fashion. We can then separate out several other types of questions: First, what induces individuals to conform to the imperative? How do individuals come to have the psychological dispositions to conform to the norm? Second, how is the norm embodied in social relations and behavior? And third, what are the social mechanisms or processes that created the imperative within the given social group? What mechanisms serve to sustain it over time?

To the first question, there seem to be only three possible answers—and each is in fact socially and psychologically possible. The imperative may be internalized into the motivational space of the individual, so he or she chooses to act according to the imperative (or is habituated to acting in such a way). There may be an effective and well-known system of sanctions that attach to violations of the norms, so the individual has an incentive to comply. These sanctions may be formal or informal. The sanction may be as benign as being laughed at for wearing a Hawaiian shirt to a black-tie ball, or as severe as being beaten for seeming liberal in a biker bar. Or, third, there may be benefits from conformance that make conformance a choice that is in the actor's rational self-interest. (Every time one demonstrates that he or she can choose the right fork for dessert, the likelihood of being invited to another formal dinner increases.) Each of these would make sense of the fact that an individual conforms his/her behavior to the requirements of a norm and helps to answer the question, why do individuals conform to norms?

The questions about the social embodiment of a norm are the most difficult. Does the embodiment of a given norm consist simply in the fact that a certain percentage of people in fact behave in accordance with the rule—for whatever reason? Does the norm exist in virtue of the fact that people consciously champion the norm and impose sanctions on violators? Might we imagine that human beings are normative animals and absorb normative systems in the way that we absorb grammatical systems—by observing and inferring about the behavior of others?

As for the third cluster of questions about genesis and persistence, there is a range of possibilities here as well. The system may have been designed by one or more deliberate actors. It may have emerged through a fairly random process that is guided by positive social feedback of some sort. It may be the resultant of multiple groups advocating for one set of norms or another to govern a given situation of conflict and/or cooperation. And, conceivably, it may be the result of something analogous to natural selection across small groups: the groups with a more efficient set of norms may out-perform competing groups.

How do individuals come to adopt norms? First, it may be that there is an effective mechanism of social education through which each individual develops or activates an internally regulative system of norms or rules. This process can be described as "moral education." The most superficial observation of social behavior indicates that this is so, and social psychologists and sociologists have some ideas about how these systems work. But the bottom line appears fairly clear: individuals who are reared in normal human settings eventually possess action-behavior systems that embody a set of personal norms that influence their conduct. We might draw the analogy to the example of language learning: a normal human child is exposed to the linguistic behavior of others, and arrives at a psychologically realized grammar that guides his/her own language production.

Second, a norm might be embodied in the attitudes, judgment, and behavior of others in such a way that their actions and reactions create incentives and disincentives for the actor. For example, others may possess a set of norms concerning civility in public discourse, and they may punish or reward others according to whether their words are consistent with these norms. In this case the agent conforms to the requirements of the norm out of a calculation of costs and benefits of performance. (It would appear that there is a possibility of circularity here: the externally imposed norm depends upon the internally embodied norm of enforcement of the content of the rule on the part of others.)

Third, it might be the case that there are some norms of inter-personal behavior that are hard-wired. Some norms might have a biological, evolutionary basis. This is the line of thought that sociobiologists have explored with varying levels of success. The emotional responses that adults have to infants and children probably fall in this category—though it is a conceptually interesting question to consider whether these emotional responses are "norms" or simply features of the affective system. This is relevant to the work that Allan Gibbard (1990) does in *Wise Choices, Apt Feelings: A Theory of Normative Judgment*. Gibbard's fundamental insight is that there must be an evolutionary basis for the "norm-acquisition system"—the features of human psychology that permit them to acquire certain kinds of moral motives (altruism, friendship, fairness). Raadschelders (2020) takes up this possibility in detail.

It seems inescapable that norms of behavior exist in a society and that individuals adjust their behavior out of regard for relevant norms. The microfoundations of how this works is obscure, however, in that we do not really have good answers to the parallel questions: how do individuals internalize norms? And how do informal practices of norm enforcement work? And what social-causal factors play a role in the emergence, persistence, and change of a system of norms at a given time?

This fact of the normative component of social action is as relevant to organizational behavior as it is to other kinds of behavior. When an individual has a commitment to the ideas of honesty and integrity, she is less likely to cheat on her expense reports. When a person recognizes the equal worth of all other human beings she is less likely to make false reports about colleagues in order to further her own career. A person's moral and normative commitments come with them into the workplace, and this is true in organizations and institutions.

But individuals are not social robots, governed entirely by their normative commitments. One of the difficult challenges in public choice theory has been to provide an account of action that allows for realistic incorporation of both normative commitment and purposive self-interest. It is plain enough that there are often conflicts between norms and self-interest, and it is clear that each individual resolves these conflicts in his or her own ways. There is also the problem of hypocrisy—the fact that individuals often publicly espouse a lofty set of norms and values, while privately behaving in ways that are directly contrary to those norms.

The same question about the need for microfoundations arises in the case of normative systems as well. Norms do not enforce themselves. So we need to be able to identify social mechanisms, embodied at the individual level, through which a specific normative system is made behaviorally effective. Here there are two broad avenues of explanation available. First is the process of socialization, and the second is the process of social enforcement.

Consider the processes of socialization. Individuals are socially constituted through an extended process of development. They usually grow up in families, in the presence of the influences of schools, teachers, worship institutions, the workplace, friendships, family, street gangs, the military, and the pub. Through these opportunities for social learning individuals internalize their own understandings of a set of social norms loosely governing behavior in social circumstances. All of these settings have institutional reality in the sense that we can provide concrete sociological description of how they work and what the mechanisms are through which a particular set of norms and values are sustained over time.

Organizational Culture

It is now broadly recognized in organizational studies that the behavior of actors within a particular organization is affected by the organization's *culture*. Two banks may have very similar organizational structures but show rather different patterns of behavior, and those differences are ascribed to differences in culture. What does this mean? Clifford Geertz is one of the most articulate theorists of culture, and he offers a clear description of religion as a cultural system (1971). A religion is...

> (1) a system of symbols which act to (2) establish powerful, pervasive, and long-lasting moods and motivations in men by (3) formulating conceptions of a general order of existence and (4) clothing these conceptions with such an aura of factuality that (5) the moods and motivations seem uniquely realistic. (Geertz 1971: 90)

And again:

> The concept of culture I espouse, and whose utility the essays below attempt to demonstrate, is essentially a semiotic one. Believing, with Max Weber, that man is an animal suspended in webs of significance he himself has spun, I take culture to be those webs, and the analysis of it to be therefore not an experimental science in search of law but an interpretive one in search of meaning. (Geertz 1971: 5)

On its face this idea seems fairly simple. We might stipulate that "culture" refers to a set of beliefs, values, and practices that are shared by a number of individuals within the group, including leaders, managers, and staff members.

Edgar Schein is a leading expert on the topic of organizational culture. Here is how he defines the concept in *Organizational Culture and Leadership* (Schein and Schein 1990). Organizational culture, according to Schein, consists of a set of "basic assumptions about the correct way to perceive, think, feel, and behave, driven by (implicit and explicit) values, norms, and ideals.... Culture is both a dynamic phenomenon that surrounds us at all times, being constantly enacted and created by our interactions with others and shaped by leadership behavior, and a set of structures, routines, rules, and norms that guide and constrain behavior" (Schein and Schein 2016: 1). According to Schein, there are cognitive and affective components of action within an organization that have little to do with rational calculation of interests and more to do with how the actors frame their choices. The values and expectations of the organization help to shape the actions of the participants. And one crucial aspect of leaders, according to Schein, is the role they play in helping to shape the culture of the organizations they lead. (Valuable insights are provided into the culture of organizations by Martin 2001 and Hofstede 2003.)

It is intriguing that several pressing organizational problems have been found to rotate around the culture of the organization within which behavior takes place. The prevalence of sexual and gender harassment appears to depend a great deal on the culture of respect and civility that an organization has embodied—or has failed to embody. The ways in which accidents occur in large industrial systems seems to depend in part on the culture of safety that has been established within the organization. And the incidence of corrupt and dishonest practices within businesses seems to be influenced by the culture of integrity that the organization has managed to create. In each instance experience seems to demonstrate that "good" culture leads to less socially harmful behavior, while "bad" culture leads to more such behavior.

The idea of safety culture has come to play a crucial role in the nuclear industry after Three Mile Island and Chernobyl. Experts both inside and outside the industry have come to understand that safe operations of a complex facility like a nuclear reactor requires a widespread culture of safety extending from top executives to managers to frontline workers. As Charles Perrow (1999) documents in detail in his analysis of Three Mile Island, accidents are all too likely in tightly coupled complex industrial processes such as a nuclear plant, and only a concerted and focused dedication to safe operations can change the odds of catastrophe.

Researchers in the area of sexual harassment have devoted quite a bit of attention to the topic of workplace culture as well. This theme is emphasized in the National Academy study on sexual and gender harassment (NASEM 2018). The authors make the point that much gender harassment is aimed at expressing disrespect towards the target rather than sexual exploitation. This has an important implication for institutional change. An institution that creates a strong core set of values emphasizing civility and respect is less conducive to gender harassment. They summarize this analysis in the statement of findings as well:

> Organizational climate is, by far, the greatest predictor of the occurrence of sexual harassment, and ameliorating it can prevent people from sexually harassing others. A person more likely to engage in harassing behaviors is significantly less likely to do so in an environment that does not support harassing behaviors and/or has strong, clear, transparent consequences for these behaviors. (50)

David Hess, an expert on corporate corruption, takes a similar approach to the problem of corruption and bribery by officials of multinational corporations (2009, 2015, 2016). Hess argues that bribery often has to do with organizational culture and individual behavior, and that effective steps to reduce the incidence of bribery must proceed on the basis of an adequate analysis of both culture and behavior. And he links this issue to fundamental problems in the area of corporate ethics within the organization. Hess believes that controlling corrupt practices requires changing incentives within the corporation while equally changing the ethical culture of the corporation; he believes that the ethical culture of a company can have effects on the degree to which employees engage in bribery and other corrupt practices.

What is in common among each of these examples is that intangible cultural features of the work environment are likely to influence behavior of the actors in that environment, and thereby affect the favorable and unfavorable outcomes of the organization's functioning as well. Moreover, if we take the lead offered by Schein and work on the assumption that leaders can influence culture through their advocacy for the values that the organization embodies, then leadership has a core responsibility to facilitate a work culture that embodies these favorable outcomes. Work culture can be cultivated to encourage safety and to discourage bad outcomes like sexual harassment and corruption.

We can ask several causal questions about this interpretation of organizational culture. What are the factors that lead to the establishment and currency of a given profile of beliefs, values, and practices within an organization? What factors exist that either reproduce those beliefs or undermine them? Finally we can ask what the consequences of a given culture profile are in the internal and external performance of the organization.

There seem to be two large causal mechanisms responsible for establishment and maintenance of a particular cultural constellation within an organization. First is recruitment. One organization may make a specific effort to screen candidates so as to select in favor of a particular set of values and attitudes—acceptance, collaboration, trustworthiness, openness to others. Another may favor attitudes and values that are thought to be more directly related to profitability or employee malleability. These selection mechanisms can lead to significant differences in the overall culture of the organization. And the decision to orient recruitment in one way rather than another is itself an expression of values.

The second large mechanism is the internal socialization and leadership processes of the organization. We can hypothesize that an organization whose leaders and supervisors both articulate the values of equality and respect in the workplace *and* who demonstrate that commitment in their own actions will be one in which more people in the organization will adopt those values. And we can likewise hypothesize that the training and evaluation processes of an organization can be effective in cultivating the values of the organization. In other words, it seems evident that leadership and training are particularly relevant to the establishment of a particular organizational culture.

The other large causal question is how and to what extent cultural differences across organizations have effects on the performance and behavior of those organizations. We can hypothesize that differences in organizational values and culture lead to differences in behavior within the organization—more or less collaboration, more or less harassment, more or less bad behavior of various kinds. These differences are themselves highly important. But we can also hypothesize that differences like these can lead to differences in organizational effectiveness. This is the central idea of the field of positive organizational studies. Scholars like Kim Cameron (2006, 2010) and others argue, on the basis of empirical studies across organizational settings, that organizations that embody the values of mutual acceptance, equality, and a positive orientation towards each others' contributions are in fact more productive organizations as well.

SOCIAL NETWORKS

Individuals bring with them a set of personal and professional relationships whenever they enter an organizational sphere, whether in government or the corporate world. They have former university classmates, friends, fellow worshippers, former work colleagues, and fellow military veterans. These relationships can be represented as a social network of interconnections. And since many of one's friends and acquaintances share relationships with the same individuals, there is a sometimes a substantial overlap across multiple actors' social networks. (Kadushin [2012] provides an accessible introduction to the fundamentals of social network theory.)

The concept of a social network brings a different kind of structure to an actor-centered theory of the social world. It is larger than a collection of individuals, in that we have to specify a set of *relationships* among individuals in order to define a social network. But it is much more concrete and agent-based than the large categories of race, class, or gender turn out to be. Robert Putnam (2000) refers to these sets of relationships as a fund of social capital. If a person needs a referral to a doctor, a reference for a business loan, or a potential fellow participant in a political effort, it will make a great deal of difference how extensive his or her social network is, and how influential and resourceful are the individuals to whom he is related. The concept of a social network thus appears to be an important component of a social ontology of government. (A good effort to link social networks theory to an important area of social science research is Mario Diani and Doug McAdam (2003), *Social Movements and Networks: Relational Approaches to Collective Action.*)

Consider the spread of boycotts in Alabama in the early 1960s which Doug McAdam describes in detail in *Political Process and the Development of Black Insurgency, 1930–1970* (1999). The boycotts had a specific dynamic of mobilization. Organizations emerged which set about to mobilize support for the strategy of boycott. Some of this effort took the form of public calls to action. But a larger part of the mobilization occurred through the workings of extended networks of engaged people—ministers, union activists, student organizations, and civil rights groups. And the effectiveness and pattern of dissemination of the call to action depended critically on the scope and structure of each of these networks of networks—networks among leaders of diverse organizations and subordinate networks clustered around each leader.

These examples lead to several observations. One is that social networks are not critical for *every* form of social action. But the exceptions are fairly simple cases of spontaneous coordination. And second, the example of civil rights mobilization illustrates very clearly why we should expect that social networks are usually crucial. The reason is straightforward: almost all social outcomes require a degree of coordination, communication, and mobilization. A social network is not the only way of bringing these factors about—cheerleaders and television stations can do it too. But the causal importance of social networks is likely to be great in many cases. Moreover, they function as bridging mechanisms from micro to macro, in that they help to convey the actions of local agents onto larger social outcomes. For this reason it is justified to conclude that social networks are in fact an important component of an adequate social ontology.

Robert Putnam (2000) referred to these relationships as "social capital" and made the important point that people differ in the amount of social capital they can bring to bear in support of their purposes. One individual has the governor, the CEO of the state's largest enterprise, and the head of the NAACP in his Rolodex; another individual has a bowling team, a set of friends from the pub, and the local priest in his corner. It is apparent that the first individual is better positioned to use his connections and friendships to his advantage than the second person.

What constitutes a social network? It is a system of the relationships that exist among individuals within a population. We can define a network in terms of multiple kinds of social relationship: communication, affinity, loyalty and obligation, economic interdependence, ethnic or religious organization, and many other kinds of social relationship. Once we have defined the kind of relationship we want to focus on, we can begin to sketch out the relationships that exist within a population with respect to this type of connection. Take communication. We might define a communication relationship between X and Y in terms of the volume of emails exchanged between them. For a given population we might then imagine a graph of the communications network of the population. Some individuals in this population are only very lightly connected to others by email; other individuals are hubs of communication who communicate with large numbers of other individuals. Here is the important point of this example. Communications networks convey messages that are socially and politically impactful. So we can analyze influence and political causation, in part, through the structure of the interpersonal communications networks that exist in a population at a time.

This question is especially important for sociologists because it goes to the heart of the reason why network maps are of sociological interest in the first place: we think that the social relationships among individuals explain important features of social action—readiness to mobilize for a political cause, for example. This intuition derives from the idea that individuals influence each other through the exchange of information and the observation of each other's behavior; and so subgroups of persons with especially dense social connections with each other may have distinctive social characteristics as a group. So identifying the communities within a social network is an important sociological discovery.

It is a feature of social capital that the relationships that are most influential often seem to involve reciprocity. Individual A can call upon individual B for support for her political campaign from the business community, and the time will come when individual B calls upon A for support in opposition to a particular plan for regulation of chemical waste.

So how do these basic facts about social capital and social networks affect the realities of government? We have seen previously that government makes decisions and affects behavior in ways that people care about, and that interested parties have strong motivations to exercise influence over the decisions and actions of governments. It is therefore instructive to examine the social networks of government officials and elected offers of government, to see whether there are indicators of potential political influence.

Several points are fairly obvious. One is that social networks do in fact constitute a key causal mechanism underlying many social processes. We can explain important features of social and political life by identifying the concrete social networks that exist within the population: the transmission of ideas, knowledge, and styles through a population; the selection of important leaders in government and industry; the effective reach of the state; the course of mobilization within a community around an important issue; and the effectiveness of a terrorist group, to name a few examples. A second point is that networks have specific features of topology and functioning that have causal consequences that are largely independent from the personal characteristics of the people who constitute it. For example, information may travel more quickly through a network of people containing many midsized nodes than one containing just a few mega-hubs. And this structural fact may suffice to explain some social outcomes: for example, this rebellion succeeded (because of rapid transmission of information) whereas that one petered out (because of ineffective communications).

So how do the analytical resources of network theory contribute to a better understanding of the ways that actions aggregate into outcomes? In his introduction to (Diani and McAdam 2003) Mario Diani emphasizes several ways in which network analysis has contributed to the study of contentious politics.

> Network analysis as it is best known developed with reference to a 'realist' view of social structure as networks which linked together concrete actors through specific ties, identifiable and measurable through reliable empirical instruments. This view represented an alternative to both views of social structures as macro forces largely independent from the control of the specific actors associated with them ...., and views of structure as aggregates of the individual actors sharing determinate specific traits. (Diani and McAdam 2003: 5)

So if we take it as a plain fact about the social world that individuals have a range of meaningful and material relationships with other individuals, both proximate and distant, then it is plainly important to understand the effects that those relationships have on their consciousness and behavior. These causal relationships are likely to extend in both directions—from the network to the actor, and from the actor back into the network.

Here is the key point: different people find themselves in very different networks of social connections, and these relationships contribute to their social and political consciousness in diverse ways. If we are interested in the spread of militant civil rights activism, as Doug McAdam (1999), or in the spread of fascist activism and mobilization in Europe in the 1920s and 1930s, as Michael Mann (2004) is in *Fascists*, it is highly relevant to discover the relationships and organizations through which individuals come into contact with each other and with the ideas of the nascent movements. Likewise, if we are interested in the proliferation of support for the Deacons of Defense in the American South in the 1950s and 1960s, as Lance Hill (2004) is, then it is important to identify the personal and organizational linkages through which ordinary people became aware of this response to white supremacy and violence. Communication of ideas and political emotions requires a mechanism connecting the "signalers" and those to whom the messages eventually percolate, and this is not a depersonalized, homogeneous process.

Recruitment and mobilization is one aspect of contentious politics where social networks are plainly important. Relationships in the workplace, the neighborhood, or the church or mosque are a likely location for the diffusion of a range of socially relevant material—news, gossip, indignation, shared views about politics. And these relationships are a potential vector for the recruitment of followers and activists for a range of new political ideas—from civil rights to Tea Party to fascism.

Identifying coalitions of collective actors is another area of current research. Once a topic has gained some degree of visibility and salience, it is likely enough that multiple groups will begin to focus on it. Anti-tax activism is a good example—dozens of "citizen-based" organizations emerged in California in the 1950s and 1960s with the overall goal of limiting property and income taxes in the state, and it is useful to track the emerging relationships that developed among these organizations and their activists.

These aspects of social networks have important implications for our topic, the ontology of government. We have seen that a government is a vast network itself of agencies and bureaus, and coordination and competition among various agencies are often brokered by personal relationships among senior and mid-level leaders. Equally importantly, the topic of the exercise of power and influence from power-holders outside of government to decision-makers inside government is often illuminated by discovery of the personal and professional relationships that exist among leaders in the broader universe of elite social life.

REFERENCES

Bates, Robert H. *Markets and States in Tropical Africa: The Political Basis of Agricultural Policies*. Berkeley: University of California Press, 1981.

Brinton, Mary C., and Victor Nee, eds. *New Institutionalism in Sociology*. New York: Russell Sage Foundation, 1998.

Cameron, Kim S. *Competing Values Leadership: Creating Value in Organizations*. New Horizons in Management. Cheltenham, UK; Northampton, MA: Edward Elgar, 2006.

Cameron, Kim S. *Organizational Effectiveness*. Cheltenham; Northhampton, MA: Edward Elgar, 2010.

Diani, Mario, and Doug McAdam, eds. *Social Movements and Networks: Relational Approaches to Collective Action*. Comparative Politics. Oxford; New York: Oxford University Press, 2003.

Geertz, Clifford. *The Interpretation of Cultures; Selected Essays*. New York: Basic Books, 1971.

Gibbard, Allan. *Wise Choices, Apt Feelings: A Theory of Normative Judgment*. Cambridge: Harvard University Press, 1990.

Hess, David J. "Catalyzing Corporate Commitment to Combating Corruption." *Journal of Business Ethics* 88 (2009): 781–90.

Hess, David J. "Combating Corruption in International Business: The Big Questions." *Ohio Northern Law Review* 41, no. 3 (2015): 679–96.

Hess, David J. "Ethical Infrastructures and Evidence-Based Corporate Compliance and Ethics Programs: Policy Implications from the Empirical Evidence." *New York University Journal of Law & Business* 12, no. 2 (2016): 317–68.

Hill, Lance E. *The Deacons for Defense: Armed Resistance and the Civil Rights Movement*. Chapel Hill: University of North Carolina Press, 2004.

Hofstede, Geert. *Culture's Consequences: Comparing Values, Behaviors, Institutions, and Organizations Across Nations*. 2nd ed. Sage, 2003.

Kadushin, Charles. *Understanding Social Networks: Theories, Concepts, and Findings*. Oxford; New York: Oxford University Press, 2012.

Knight, Jack. *Institutions and Social Conflict*. The Political Economy of Institutions and Decisions. Cambridge, UK; New York, NY: Cambridge University Press, 1992.

Mahoney, James, and Kathleen Ann Thelen. *Explaining Institutional Change: Ambiguity, Agency, and Power*. Cambridge; New York: Cambridge University Press, 2010.

Mann, Michael. *Fascists*. New York: Cambridge University Press, 2004.

Martin, Joanne. *Organizational Culture: Mapping the Terrain (Foundations for Organizational Science)*. Joanne Martin: Sage, 2001.

McAdam, Doug. *Political Process and the Development of Black Insurgency, 1930–1970*. 2nd ed. Chicago: University of Chicago Press, 1999.

National Academies of Sciences, Engineering, and Medicine. *Sexual Harassment of Women: Climate, Culture, and Consequences in Academic Sciences, Engineering, and Medicine*. Washington, DC: The National Academies Press, 2018. https://doi.org/10.17226/24994.

Ocasio, William, Patricia H. Thornton, and Michael Lounsbury. "Advances to the Institutional Logics Perspective." In *Sage Handbook of Organizational Institutionalism*. 2nd ed. London; Thousand Oaks, CA: Sage, 2017.

Ostrom, Elinor. *Governing the Commons: The Evolution of Institutions for Collective Action*. Cambridge, UK; New York: Cambridge University Press, 1990.

Perrow, Charles. *Normal Accidents: Living with High-Risk Technologies—With a New Afterword and a Postscript on the Y2K Problem*. Princeton, NJ: Princeton University Press, 1999 [1984].

Pierson, Paul. *Politics in Time: History, Institutions, and Social Analysis*. Princeton: Princeton University Press, 2004.

Powell, Walter, and Paul J. DiMaggio. *The New Institutionalism in Organizational Analysis*. Chicago: University of Chicago Press, 1991.

Putnam, Robert D. *Bowling Alone: The Collapse and Revival of American Community*. New York: Simon & Schuster, 2000.

Raadschelders, Jos C. N. *What Is Government? Human Instinct, Tribal Community, Global Society*. Ann Arbor: University of Michigan Press, 2020.

Schein, Edgar, and Peter Schein. *Organizational Culture and Leadership*. 5th ed. New York: Jossey-Bass, 2016 [1990].

Sen, Amartya. "Rational Fools: A Critique of the Behavioral Foundations of Economic Theory." *Philosophy & Public Affairs* 6, no. 4 (1977): 317–44.

Thelen, Kathleen, and James Conran. "Institutional Change." In *The Oxford Handbook of Historical Institutionalism*, edited by Orfeo Fioretos, Tulia G. Falleti, and Adam Sheingate. Oxford; New York: Oxford University Press, 2016.

Thelen, Kathleen Ann. *How Institutions Evolve: The Political Economy of Skills in Germany, Britain, the United States, and Japan*. Cambridge Studies in Comparative Politics. Cambridge; New York: Cambridge University Press, 2004.

Thornton, Patricia H., and William Ocasio. "Institutional Logics." In *The SAGE Handbook of Organizational Institutionalism*, edited by Royston Greenwood, Christine Oliver, Roy Suddaby, and Kerstin Sahlin-Andersson, 1st ed. Thousand Oaks, CA: Sage, 2008.

Thornton, Patricia H., William Ocasio, and Michael Lounsbury. *The Institutional Logics Perspective: A New Approach to Culture, Structure, and Process*. Oxford: Oxford University Press, 2012.

CHAPTER 6

Sources of Organizational Failure

Abstract This chapter turns to the sources of failure and dysfunction that arise within existing organizations. If organizations were automata governed by exceptionless rules and procedures, the world we live in would be very different. All the individuals within the organization would fulfill the assignments of their roles, and the organization would function fully as designed. However, individuals are not automata, and their interests, plans, understandings, and priorities commonly diverge in various ways from the organization's designs. The chapter considers the social realities of conflict of interest, loose coupling, principal-agent problems, and failures of communication as sources of organizational dysfunction. The chapter focuses on a key consequence of the social realities of government presented to this point: the fact that agencies and bureaucracies represent loosely-linked groups of actors who have a variety of different interests, only imperfectly subject to control by the central executive.

Keywords Compliance · Conflict of interest · Corruption · Dysfunction · Loose coupling · Principal-agent problem

If organizations were automata governed by algorithms, the world we live in would be very different. All the individuals within the organization would fulfill the assignments of their roles, at the maximum of their ability and energy, and the organization would function fully as designed. There are two major ways in which the world differs from this idea. First, individuals are not transistors; they are actors, with their own reasons and motives for action. So we cannot assume that their actions will be a straightforward expression of their roles and assignments. And second, organizations are not examples of perfect and flawless design. Instead, it is frequent enough to find one subsystem whose functions lead it into conflict with the functioning of another subsystem (Clarke and Perrow 1996; Anheier 1999; Bovens and 't Hart 2017; de Vries 2010).

This chapter focuses on a key consequence of the social realities of government presented to this point: the fact that agencies and bureaucracies represent loosely-linked groups of actors who have a variety of different interests, only imperfectly subject to control by the central executive. This is the key theme of the "natural systems" approach to organizations described in Chapter 4. This unavoidable looseness of bureaucratic organization creates the possibility of several kinds of lack of coherence between government's intentions and the actual activities of agencies and departments. The chapter introduces the idea of a principal-agent problem and demonstrates that this is an unavoidable feature of organizational functioning. It also applies the idea of "loose coupling" to the challenges associated with inter-agency collaboration. And it touches on an important problem at the level of the actor, the problem of conflict of interest and commitment. The chapter considers a range of organizational mechanisms aimed at enhancing internal controls and compliance.

Government does many things quite well. It also contains familiar dysfunctions and failures: failure to exercise regulatory scrutiny, lax enforcement, inter-agency conflict, systematic miscalculation of consequences, failure to accept uncomfortable scientific facts, corruption and conflict of interest, and so on. This chapter seeks to locate some of the origins of dysfunction within the kinds of factors identified in prior chapters. Function and dysfunction are associated with the same underlying features of organizational life we have examined previously. The chapter considers several organizational mechanisms through which various common dysfunctions can be addressed. The influence of powerful outsider stakeholders is a common source of dysfunction (in the implementation of the regulations of the Nuclear Regulatory Commission, for example). The fact of principal-agent problems throughout the extended organization is another important source of dysfunction.

And failures of communication and coordination inherent in the loosely connected structure of government is another.

These topics are important for our central concern for the ontology of government because they have to do with limiting features of governmental unity of action and effectiveness that derive from the fundamental nature of social interaction and organization. We have seen that social entities, processes, and causal powers derive from the features of the individual actors who make them up. The actors behave in various ways within the setting of rules, expectations, demands, norms, and guidelines that constitute the institutional environment in which they act. But their actions are never algorithmic or automatic. Rather (as we have seen in the discussion of strategic action fields and other treatments of institutions) individual actors have their own states of agency—goals and motivations, belief frameworks, normative schemes that are separate from the organizational setting. So we can count on the fact that there will always be actions and patterns of behavior within an institution or organization that derive from private motives rather than organizational imperatives, and there will be well-intentioned conflicts of goals within the organization as well. These occasions of non-sanctioned behavior do not necessarily fall in the category of corruption or theft; but they create the unavoidable possibility that the actions of the organization, through the actions of various individuals within the organization, will deviate from those intended by the leaders and executives and will be substantially less unified than one might wish.

These problems are perhaps analogous to the issues that arise in a manufacturing process when friction within a machine, improperly tooled parts, or parts that are prone to breaking all lead to defective products. These kinds of failures are inherent in any real physical process. No machine functions entirely as its blueprints prescribe, and no organization functions entirely as its organization chart and formal operating procedures prescribe.

Dysfunction

Organizations make serious mistakes; and those mistakes often occur because of systemic features of the organization itself or its components. Organizational dysfunction is a persistent reality. The Nuclear Regulatory Commission failed to discover and address extensive dangerous corrosion in the Davis-Besse nuclear plant (U.S. Government Accountability Office

2004). American intelligence agencies failed to recognize the importance of a number of available pieces of information in the months preceding the September 11 attacks. The State of Michigan erroneously identified thousands of unemployment claims in the financial crisis of 2008 as fraudulent and automatically assessed large penalties against innocent people. The French army persistently misjudged the military risk at Dien Bien Phu. In each of these cases, and myriad other available examples, large organizations made crucial and consequential mistakes in areas central to their missions.

When we examine large failures and disasters our attention is often drawn to the specific individual mistakes that were made. But in the background we almost always find organizations and practices through which complex technical activities are designed, implemented, and regulated. Human actors, organized into patterns of cooperation, collaboration, competition, and command, are as crucial to technical processes as are power lines, cooling towers, and control systems in computers. So it is imperative that we follow the lead of researchers like Charles Perrow (1999), Kathleen Tierney (2014), or Diane Vaughan (1996) and give close attention to the social- and organization-level failures that sometimes lead to massive organizational failures.

Think of the range of disasters and failures that have occurred in the past several decades within large organizations, both private and public: Three Mile Island, Chernobyl, and Fukushima; the Challenger and Columbia space shuttle disasters; fatal flaws in the DC-10, Osprey, and Boeing 737 MAX aircraft design processes; the failure of Federal land use and flood insurance policies in flood-prone areas; the failure of FEMA to provide adequate disaster relief following Hurricane Katrina; and continuing examples of hospital-born infections and accidents in some hospitals. Careful studies of each of these disasters demonstrates that organizational shortcomings played important roles in the occurrence of the accidents and their aftermath.

Examples like these allow us to begin to create an inventory of organizational flaws that sometimes lead to costly failures and accidents. Here are a few key examples of organizational failures that show up in multiple instances of large-scale failure: vulnerability to influence by powerful outsiders; excessive management concern for profitability and cost-cutting; production pressures that lead to reduced attention to safety; siloed decision-making; lack of high-level officials responsible for safety and compliance; lax implementation of formal processes; strategic bureaucratic manipulation of outcomes; poor internal communications; poor training and supervision; poor planning for failure scenarios; information withholding and lying; corrupt practices, conflicts of interest and commitment; short-term calculation of costs and benefits by decision-makers; indifference to public goods; and poor gathering and evaluation of mission-relevant data. All of these defects can contribute to failures, both small and large.

What is a *dysfunction* when it comes to the normal workings of an organization? In order to identify dysfunctions we need to have a prior conception of the "purpose" or "agreed-upon goals" of an organization. Fiscal agencies collect taxes; child protective services work to ensure that foster children are placed in safe and nurturing environments; air travel safety regulators ensure that aircraft and airfields meet high standards of maintenance and operations; drug manufacturers produce safe, high-quality medications at a reasonable cost. A dysfunction might be defined as a process within an organization or institution that leads to results that are significantly contrary to the purpose of the organization. We can think of major failures in each of these examples. But we need to make a distinction between failure and dysfunction. The latter concept is systemic, having to do with the design and culture of the organization. Failure can happen as a result of dysfunctional arrangements; but it can happen as a result of other kinds of factors as well. For example, the Tylenol crisis of 1982 resulted from malicious tampering by an external third party, not organizational dysfunction.

But—as in software development—it is sometimes difficult to distinguish between a feature and a bug. What is dysfunctional for the public may indeed be beneficial for other actors who are in a position to influence the design and workings of the organization—executives, shareholders, governing boards, supervisors, frontline workers. This is the key finding of researchers like Jack Knight (1992), who argues for the prevalence of conflicting interests in the design and operations of many institutions and organizations. And it follows immediately from the approach to organizations encapsulated in the Fligstein and McAdam theory of strategic action fields considered in Chapter 4.

There is another important question to consider: why do recognized dysfunctional characteristics persist? When a piano is out of tune, the pianist and the audience insist on a professional tuning. When the

Nuclear Regulatory Commission persistently fails to enforce its regulations through rigorous inspection protocols, nothing happens. Is it that the individuals responsible for the day-to-day functioning of the organization are complacent or unmotivated? Is it that there are contrary pressures that arise to oppose corrective action? Or, sometimes, is it that the adjustments needed to correct one set of dysfunctions can be expected to create another, even more harmful, set of bad outcomes?

It is possible to identify several possible causes of the persistence of organizational defects. The first is that a dysfunction from one point of view may well be a desirable feature from another point of view. The lack of an authoritative safety officer in a chemical plant may be thought to be dysfunctional if we are thinking about the safety of workers and the public as a primary goal of the plant. But if profitability and cost-savings are the primary goals from the point of view of the stakeholders, then the cost-benefit analysis may favor the omission of the safety officer. Second, there may be internal failures within an organization that are beyond the reach of any executive or manager who might want to correct them. The complexity and loose-coupling of large organizations militate against house cleaning on a large scale. Third, there may be powerful factions within an organization for whom the "dysfunctional" feature is an important component of their own set of purposes and goals. Fligstein and McAdam argue for this kind of disaggregation with their theory of strategic action fields. By disaggregating purposes and goals to the various actors who figure in the life cycle of the organization—founders, stakeholders, executives, managers, experts, frontline workers, labor organizers—it is possible to see the organization as a whole as the complex aggregation of the multiple actions and purposes of the actors within and adjacent to the organization. This aggregation does not imply that the organization is carefully adjusted to serve the public good or to maximize efficiency or to protect the health and safety of the public. Rather, it suggests that the resultant organizational structure serves the interests of the various actors to the fullest extent each actor is able to manage.

Let us consider some specific behavioral features of organizational life that are conducive to dysfunctional processes and outcomes.

Principal-Agent Problems

Organizations (and all other forms of extended social cooperation) are subject to the reality that the interests of the actors within the organization are to varying degrees distinct from the wishes and directives of the executive of the group, and the supervisory powers of the executive are limited. For example, a regional tax official in Manila wants the local tax assessors to provide honest assessments of the quality of farmland in their districts, but local assessors sometimes accept small gifts from farmers in exchange for a lower-than-justified assessment. A bishop in the capital city wants the village priests to encourage young parishioners to refrain from dancing on Saturday nights; some of the priests omit this message because of their wish for good relations with the families in the village. The construction manager for a large project wants the skilled workers on the project to work intensively for the duration of the work day, but the skilled workers find ways of reducing their actual work time to only a few hours. Each of these cases illustrates what social scientists refer to as a "principal-agent" problem: a separation between the wishes and expectations of the executive and the purposeful actions of his or her agent.

A principal-agent problem is a situation in which an authority (the principal) instructs a subordinate (the agent) to complete a task, but where the principal has limited ability to monitor and supervise the agent's performance. The agent may exercise his or her activities in accordance with his own preferences rather than the principal's instructions. Here is a good description of the principal-agent problem by Joseph Stiglitz:

> A principal-agent problem arises when there is imperfect information, either concerning what action the agent has undertaken or what he should undertake. In many situations, the actions of an individual are not easily observable. It would be very difficult for a landlord to monitor perfectly the weeding activity of his tenant. A bank cannot monitor perfectly the actions of those to whom it lends money. The employer cannot travel on the road with his salesman, to monitor precisely the effort he puts into his salesmanship. In each of these situations, the agent's (tenant's, borrower's, employee's) action affect the principal (landlord, lender, employer). Clearly, if an individual's actions are unobservable, then compensation cannot be based on those actions. (Stiglitz 1989: 241)

How does an organization assure that its agents perform their duties truthfully and faithfully? We have ample evidence of the other kind of performance—theft, misappropriation, lies, fraud, diversion of assets for personal use, and a variety of deceptive accounting schemes. And we have whole professions devoted to detecting and punishing these various forms of dishonesty—accountants, investigative reporters, management consultants, insurance experts, prosecutors and their investigators. And yet non-compliant behavior is common, in business, finance, government, and non-profit and faith-based organizations.

The examples mentioned here have to do with conflicting economic interests between principal and agent, but the problem is more general than that. The differences of motive that exist between principal and agent may be ideological or moral as easily as economic, and they may involve differences of factual judgment as well. A university administrator may believe that students are academically best served by enrolling for 15 credit hours per semester; the academic advisors who directly interact with students may believe that for most students it is better for them to take only 12 hours, and give advice accordingly. This divergence is not explained by an economic interest on the part of the advisor, but rather a moral and factual disagreement between advisor and administrator.

Collective or coordinated actions in which there are significant principal-agent problems often result in outcomes that diverge significantly from the principal's intentions.

Loose Coupling

Government functions through agencies and coordination among agencies. Consequently many purposes of government must be achieved through "inter-agency collaboration". It is a feature of a group of organizations that have dealings with each other that they may be loosely or tightly coupled. Tightly coupled groups of organizations have a high level of coordination, dense communication, protocols establishing authority relations and terms of cooperation, and established relationships among personnel in both organizations. Loosely coupled groups of organizations have the contrary properties. The have weak protocols defining the terms of cooperation, often weak and intermittent communication, and a consequently low level of effective collaboration. Management theorists have argued that there are strengths associated with loosely coupled organizations, including a greater ability to innovate and adapt in a changing environment. Orton and Weick (1990) provide a review of the literature and attempt a degree of conceptual clarification of the concept of loose coupling. But when it comes to coordination of decisions and actions across separate organizations, it would appear that loose coupling is a prescription for failure. In Weick's (1976) original formulation the concept was applied to sub-units within an organization, but the concept is also useful as a way of analyzing the functional relationships among organizations that need to collaborate in order to bring about a desired outcome (Orton and Weick 1990: 208, Scott and Davis 2007: 94). "Tightly coupled systems are portrayed as having responsive components that do not act independently, whereas loosely coupled systems are portrayed as having independent components that do not act responsively" (Orton and Weick 1990: 205).

Loose coupling can derive from several sources. Weak communication is a common source of loosely coupled organizations. Agency A is charged with accomplishing X. It has done fact-discovery to arrive at a plan for how to achieve X. This plan needs coordinated behavior from Agency B at multiple points. Coordination may fail to occur if A is unable to accurately and regularly share information with B. A second source of loose coupling has to do with conflicting priorities. All effort requires the expenditure of effort and resources. A's request to B to perform several support tasks in pursuit of X may be met with B's response that it cannot afford to do all of these tasks. Or B may simply "slow-walk" the process, leaving A chronically underprepared for the next step of its plan. If we take it for granted that X is in the interest of the government as a whole, the optimal outcome is one where A and B fully communicate, collaborate, and provide appropriate resources for achieving the outcome. But this ideal outcome is unlikely to occur when A and B are very loosely coupled.

The field of government is rich with illustrations of the reality of loose coupling. Many important government problems require the activities and coordination of multiple large agencies, each with its own decision structure and modes of operation. Successful performance of the overall goal requires coordination of effort; but that coordination can rarely be achieved by fiat. The example of US anti-submarine warfare in 1942 is a good example, with multiple commands within two major services (Navy and Army) each asserting separate and independent authority for action. The result was an exceptionally poor performance in attacking and destroying German submarines in US coastal waters (Cohen and Gooch 1990).

These observations suggest that government is rife with loose coupling. But so are large business organizations like General Motors, Google, or JPMorgan Chase. Each corporation consists of multiple divisions, and each division has its own mission and business objectives. The corporation's plans and goals can only be achieved through a degree of coordination and collaboration among the divisions; but often that collaboration is difficult to achieve. The manufacturing division and the marketing division have different interests; each has needs that the other can best satisfy; and achieving the desired level of cooperation is often challenging. Here is an example of this factor in the Ford Motor Company, a large and generally well-managed corporation.

> Ford had a long tradition of rapidly cycling executives through new posts every two years or so. In fact, managers used to refer to their posts as "assignments" rather than jobs. One consequence was that managers needed to make their goals in a short time period. This discouraged cooperation with other divisions and regions, whose products were often on a different timetable. Also engineers did not get rewarded or recognized for carrying over their predecessor's design or idea—even if it saved big money. (Hellriegel and Slocum 2009: 486)

Conflict of Interest

Organizations assign individual actors to roles, and these roles define specific duties and responsibilities for the individuals who occupy them. These duties incorporate the defining mission and interests of the organization itself, as well as more specific mission and interests associated with the particular division and role within which the individual serves. An actor possesses a conflict of interest when he or she has economic, financial, or personal interests that would lead him or her act in ways contrary to the duties defined by the role. Here is how ethicist Dennis Thompson defines conflict of interest: "A conflict of interest is a set of conditions in which professional judgment concerning a primary interest (such as a patient's welfare or the validity of research) tends to be unduly influenced by a secondary interest (such as financial gain). Conflict-of-interest rules, informal and formal, regulate the disclosure and avoidance of these conditions" (Thompson 1993: 573). This statement is formulated with regard to medicine and academic professional life, but it is entirely applicable to behavior within government and private organizations as well.

Consider an example from the medical system. A physician within a hospital system is obligated to serve the interests of her patients first and foremost. The physician is also expected to act in accordance with the mission of the hospital as a formal organization. Suppose, however, that the physician also owns a part of a medical imaging company and refers her patients to receive X-rays from this company. This is a potential conflict of interest, because the physician receives financial benefits from the referral, and we cannot be certain whether the referral was guided, first, by the patient's best interests, and second, by the policies of the hospital, or instead by the private financial interests that are also present. Or consider a high administrator in the Food and Drug Administration who also owns substantial stock in a pharmaceutical company. In the absence of effective regulations concerning conflict of interest, there is always the possibility that the administrator will favor policies that enhance the stock of the company, rather than being guided by the expectations and responsibilities of his role. Marc Rodwin's (2011) treatment of medical conflict of interest provides a clear formulation of the material situation that creates the possibility or likelihood of conflicts of interest in medicine and the hazards this creates for patients.

Virtually all organizations have formal policies designed to handle conflict of interest, with the ultimate goal of ensuring that decisions and actions within the organization will be guided by the values, goals, and interests of the organization rather than the private interests of the actors within the organization. The most common avenue of regulation is to require disclosure of potential conflicts and the creation of a conflict-management plan that ensures that private interests are not introduced into the decision-making of the organization. There are positive measures as well. Organizations can do quite a bit to encourage ethical behavior as part of the culture of the organization.

Is it possible to eliminate the possibility of conflict of interest altogether? Certainly not, because it is inherent in the nature of a purposive actor to have a range of motives, interests, commitments, and priorities. Some of those commitments are role-defined (public), and others are private. The idea of a "selfless" executive or official is untenable on its face. It goes without saying that many, perhaps the great majority, of officials and other actors within organizations bring a set of ethical commitments to their work, and most of those probably succeed in placing their ethical obligations of role responsibilities ahead of their financial interests. But that does not mean that the conflicts do not exist.

Corruption

Let us turn now to explicit corruption within an organization. Robert Klitgaard is an expert on the institutional causes of corruption in various social arrangements. His book *Controlling Corruption* (1988) laid out several case studies in detail, demonstrating specific features of institutional design that either encouraged or discouraged corrupt behavior by social and political actors. More recently Klitgaard prepared a major report for the OECD on the topic of corruption and development assistance (2015). This working paper offers a great deal of insight into the dysfunctional origins of corruption as an institutional fact. Here is a statement of the kinds of institutional facts that lead to higher levels of corruption: "Corruption is a crime of calculation. Information and incentives alter patterns of corruption. Processes with strong monopoly power, wide discretion for officials and weak accountability are prone to corruption…. Corruption can go beyond bribery to include nepotism, neglect of duty and favouritism. Corrupt acts can involve third parties outside the organisation (in transactions with clients and citizens, such as extortion and bribery) or be internal to an organisation (theft, embezzlement, some types of fraud). Corruption can occur in government, business, civil society organisations and international agencies. Each of these varieties has the dimension of scale, from episodic to systemic" (Klitgaard 2015: 7, 18).

The bulk of Klitgaard's report is devoted to outlining mechanisms through which governments, international agencies, and donor agencies can attempt to initiate effective reform processes leading to lower levels of corruption. There are two theoretical foundations underlying the recommendations, one having to do with the internal factors that enhance or reduce corruption and the other having to do with a theory of effective institutional change. The internal theory is couched as a piece of algebra: corruption is the result of monopoly power plus official discretion minus accountability (2015: 37). So effective interventions should be designed around reducing monopoly power and official discretion while increasing accountability.

A more micro-level perspective on international corruption is provided by a recent study by David Hess (2015). Hess focuses on the Foreign Corrupt Practices Act in the United States, and he asks the question, why do large corporations pay bribes when this is clearly illegal under the FCPA? Moreover, given that FCPA has the power to assess very large fines against corporations that violate its strictures, how can violation be a rational strategy? Hess considers the case of Siemens, which was fined over $1.5 billion in 2008 for repeated acts of bribery in the pursuit of contracts (Hess 2015: 3). He considers two theories of corporate bribing: a cost-benefit analysis showing that the practice of bribing leads to higher returns, and the "rogue employee" view, according to which the corporation is unable to control the actions of its occasionally unscrupulous employees. On the latter view, bribery is essentially a principal-agent problem.

Hess takes the position that bribery often has to do with organizational culture and individual behavior, and that effective steps to reduce the incidence of bribery must proceed on the basis of an adequate analysis of both culture and behavior. And he links this issue to fundamental problems in the area of corporate social responsibility. Hess believes that controlling corrupt practices requires changing incentives within the corporation while equally changing the ethical culture of the corporation; he believes that the ethical culture of a company can have effects on the degree to which employees engage in bribery and other corrupt practices.

The study of corruption is an ideal case for the general topic of institutional dysfunction. And, as many countries have demonstrated, it is remarkably difficult to alter the pattern of corrupt behavior in a large, complex government and society.

Accountability and Compliance Mechanisms

These related social mechanisms involving actors within organizations all lead to imperfect organizational behavior, and sometimes to behavior that is dysfunctional to the point of complete failure. But much of organizational science and management theory is directed precisely to the challenge of creating buffers against these individual-level dysfunctions. The most obvious is the process of work supervision that is part of virtually every work environment. Supervisors are given the responsibility of ensuring that each worker is working at the level of quality and intensity expected for the job. Intricate processes of performance evaluation are created and implemented, with the goal of assessing work quality. (Naturally, the issue of principal-agent problems arises here as well: supervisors too are subject to perverse incentives and may perform their jobs in ways their own executives did not intend.)

Second, every organization have accounting and audit functions that are designed to make business misconduct more difficult to carry off. The process of contracts and purchasing is a particularly fertile location for financial misconduct and the exercise of conflict of interest; so elaborate procedures are created to ensure that multiple individuals must sign off on contracts and purchases; that major purchases must be publicly presented for bid; and that there are mechanisms for verifying compliance with financial processes like expense reports.

Third, organizations make special efforts to gain compliance with conflict-of-interest policy, including the requirement of annual COI reports by officers and managers. These efforts have received new impetus in the healthcare industry as a result of heightened public awareness of the intertwining that has existed between pharmaceutical companies and healthcare professionals, practitioners, and researchers.

In *Administrative Behavior* Herbert Simon (1997) addresses these key organizational challenges. He refers to several kinds of influence that executives and supervisors exercise over workers: formal authority (enforced by the power to hire and fire), organizational loyalty (cultivated through specific means within the organization), and training. Simon holds that a crucial role of administrative leadership is the task of motivating the employees of the organization to carry out the organization's plans efficiently and effectively. He refers to five "mechanisms of organization influence" through which noncompliance and misbehavior can be reduced (Simon 1997: 112): specialization and division of task; the creation of standard practices; transmission of decisions downwards through authority and influence; channels of communication in all directions; and training and indoctrination. Through these mechanisms the executive seeks to ensure a high level of conformance and efficient performance of tasks.

Perhaps most fundamentally, organizations are well advised to cultivate a culture of ethical behavior among its participants, with high expectations for all actors, top to bottom, in terms of their standards of ethics and integrity (Hess 2009). It is certainly true that such an effort will not succeed if the behavior of leaders is visibly short of those standards. But sincere and consistent efforts on the part of organization leaders advocating for the values of honesty and integrity go a long way to creating an environment in which principal-agent problems, corruption, and conflict of interest are much less common.

Solutions for principal-agent problems are somewhat more circuitous, because by definition the knowledge available to the principal about the behavior and performance of the agent is limited. Supervision systems are difficult or impossible. Here a range of more indirect systems for governing principal-agent discrepancies has been developed. For example, profit-sharing and sales commissions have the effect of realigning the behavior of the elusive sales representative. If she is especially effective in her job through diligence and effort, the company will benefit, revenues will rise, and her own compensation will eventually share in this benefit.

How Do These Factors Apply to Government?

These factors are intimately relevant to the workings of government and public administration. Begin with conflict of interest. Given the size of government, the number of agencies it encompasses, and the army of individuals who are empowered to make decisions and give authoritative advice, there is a perennial possibility of conflict of interest and self-dealing.

The fact of loose coupling is less likely to cause headlines but is an unmistakable source of dysfunction in government. One agency sets about the goal of achieving X; another agency pursues Y which is incompatible with X. Information is hoarded by one agency or the other; there is a lack of *communication* about strategies; and collaboration is impaired or rendered entirely impossible.

Principal-agent problems are likewise a permanent part of the processes of government and public administration. Some Federal agencies appear to be more centralized than others, but examples of senior regional officials of an agency who appear to be working at cross-purposes with their executives in Washington are numerous.

Loose coupling and poor communications are also endemic possibilities within a large, complex government. One agency has the charter to monitor ground-water quality nationally; another agency has some of the equipment needed to perform regular monitoring. Without effective coordination and communication the monitoring agency's work will be ineffective.

The realities of principal-agent problems, loose coupling, conflicts of interest, and other unavoidable features of social coordination underline a fundamental limitation of the capacity of organizations and governments to behave in fully intentional and unitary ways. There is an unavoidable slippage between the mission of the organization, the actions and decisions of the executives, and the actions of the agents of the organization at every level of the organizational chart.

Further, it is crucial to note that government embodies a number of institutions intended to correct for these dysfunctions and deviations. For example, the Government Accountability Office (GAO) prepares special investigations, testimonials, and reports in response to Congressional request, requests from heads of Federal agencies, and public complaints. The GAO is the Federal government's primary audit agency, but Federal agencies also maintain their own Inspector General offices which are charged with preventing waste, fraud, mismanagement, and illegal practices, and with responding to whistle-blower complaints. The Federal Office of Government Ethics is responsible for applying Federal conflict of interest laws and policies within government agencies. The OGE describes its mission in these terms: "The U.S. Office of Government Ethics (OGE) oversees the executive branch ethics program and works with a community of ethics practitioners made up of nearly 5,000 ethics officials in more than 130 agencies to implement that program. When government decisions are made free from conflicts of interest, the public can have greater confidence in the integrity of executive branch programs and operations. OGE's mission is part of a system of institutional integrity in the executive branch."

These observations should not be understood to support the sometimes strident view that government is inherently incapable of acting coherently in the public interest. This is certainly not the case. Rather, the point is that *every* human institution—public, private, spiritual, charitable, voluntary, military, or educational—is made up of individuals who have their own states of agency and their own goals and preferences, and it is impossible for an organizational structure to function as an idealized and unitary "machine" of collective activity. Instead, the leaders must attempt to create organizational and motivational arrangements that work best to minimize the dysfunctional propensities created by these facts of disunity. This is the credo of the school of organizational studies called the theory of high-reliability organizations: "The common assumption of the high reliability theorists is not a naive belief in the ability of human beings to behave with perfect rationality, it is the much more plausible belief that organizations, properly designed and managed, can compensate for well-known human frailties and can therefore be significantly more rational and effective than can individuals" (Sagan 1993: 16). Sagan summarizes some of the key findings advanced by researchers studying "high-reliability organizations" (16–17), and some of these finding seem to be relevant for government agencies as well.

The application to government action, agency, and decision-making is straightforward: policy-makers need to be aware of the dysfunctions that are always lurking in the intricacies of organizations, and to take steps to minimize their negative consequences. This means that regulatory agencies need to ensure adequate and independent inspections of facilities, advisory panels need to take steps to avoid conflicts of interest in its expert advisors, and legislators need to write legislation mindful of the distorting effects of industry advocacy.

These observations are all relevant to the conduct of organizations, large and small. But how are they relevant to our fundamental topic here, the ontology of government? The answer is that we will have fundamentally misunderstood the nature of the entities, forces, and structures that make up government if we are unaware of the unavoidable workings of the kinds of issues raised in this chapter. In this sense these organizational deficiencies are part of the "stuff" of the world of government and all other forms of social organization. Like friction or entropy in the natural world, they are processes that are interwoven with the fabric of social organization and that cannot be fully eliminated. An adequate social ontology of government must take account of these characteristic features of agents within organizations and collective actions.

In the next several chapters we turn our attention to specific features of government action and deliberation that warrant our attention in consideration of the features of social coordination and authority that this view of social actors within organizations entails. In Chapter 7 we consider some of the collective challenges presented by an electoral representative process in constituting a government. Chapter 8 considers the "doings and thinking processes" of government, acknowledging the cognitive and practical limitations of large organizations. And Chapter 9 considers the challenges that government faces in enforcing its will upon powerful non-governmental actors, through a consideration of the purpose and limitations of government regulation of industry.

References

Anheier, Helmut K., ed. *When Things Go Wrong: Organizational Failures and Breakdowns*. Thousand Oaks, CA: Sage, 1999.
Bovens, Mark, and Paul 't Hart. *Understanding Policy Fiascoes*. London: Routledge, 2017.
Clarke, Lee, and Charles Perrow. "Prosaic Organizational Failure." *American Behavioral Scientist* 39, no. 8 (1996): 1040–56.
Cohen, Eliot, and John Gooch. *Military Misfortunes: The Anatomy of Failure in War*. New York: Vintage, 1990.
De Vries, Michiel S. *The Importance of Neglect in Policy-Making*. London; New York: Palgrave Macmillan, 2010.
Hellriegel, Don, and John W. Slocum. *Organizational Behavior*. 12th ed. Mason, OH: South-Western Cengage Learning, 2009.
Hess, David J. "Catalyzing Corporate Commitment to Combating Corruption." *Journal of Business Ethics* 88 (2009): 781–90.
Hess, David J. "Combating Corruption in International Business: The Big Questions." *Ohio Northern Law Review* 41, no. 3 (2015): 679–96.
Klitgaard, Robert E. *Controlling Corruption*. Berkeley: University of California Press, 1988.
Klitgaard, Robert E. *Addressing Corruption Together*. Paris: OECD Development Centre, 2015.
Knight, Jack. *Institutions and Social Conflict*. The Political Economy of Institutions and Decisions. Cambridge, UK; New York, NY: Cambridge University Press, 1992.
Orton, J. Douglas, and Karl E. Weick. "Loosely Coupled Systems: A Reconceptualization." *Academy of Management Review* 15, no. 2 (1990): 203–23.
Perrow, Charles. *Normal Accidents: Living with High-Risk Technologies—With a New Afterword and a Postscript on the Y2K Problem*. Princeton, NJ: Princeton University Press, 1999 [1984].
Rodwin, Marc. *Conflicts of Interest and the Future of Medicine in the United States, France, and Japan*. Oxford; New York: Oxford University Press, 2011.
Sagan, Scott Douglas. *The Limits of Safety: Organizations, Accidents, and Nuclear Weapons*. Princeton, NJ: Princeton University Press, 1993.
Scott, W. Richard, and Gerald F. Davis. *Organizations and Organizing: Rational, Natural, and Open System Perspectives*. 1st ed. Upper Saddle River, NJ: Pearson Prentice Hall, 2007.
Simon, Herbert A. *Administrative Behavior: A Study of Decision-Making Processes in Administrative Organizations*. 4th ed. New York: Free Press, 1997 [1947].
Stiglitz, Joseph E. "Principal and Agent." In *Allocation, Information and Markets*, edited by John Eatwell, Murray Milgate, and Peter Newman, 241–53. The New Palgrave. London: Palgrave Macmillan, 1989.

Thompson, Dennis F. "Understanding Financial Conflicts of Interest." *New England Journal of Medicine* 329, no. 8 (1993): 573–76.

Tierney, Kathleen J. *The Social Roots of Risk Producing Disasters, Promoting Resilience.* Stanford, CA: Stanford Business Books, an imprint of Stanford University Press, 2014.

US Government Accountability Office. *Nuclear Regulation: NRC Needs to More Aggressively and Comprehensively Resolve Issues Related to the Davis-Besse Nuclear Power Plant's Shutdown.* Washington, DC: U.S. Government, 2004. www.gao.gov/cgi-bin/getrpt?GAO-04-415.

Vaughan, Diane. *The Challenger Launch Decision: Risky Technology, Culture, and Deviance at NASA.* Chicago: University of Chicago Press, 1996.

Weick, Karl E. "Educational Organizations as Loosely Coupled Systems." *Administrative Science Quarterly* 21, no. 1 (1976): 1–19.

CHAPTER 7

Electoral Democracy

Abstract Government within a democracy is expected to reflect the will of the people. However, the institutional arrangements of liberal democracy create the possibility of significant lack of alignment between government action and the public good. The political power of the electorate is offset by the political power and influence wielded by interested parties. Lobbying, corporate influence on legislation and regulation, manipulation of the electoral process by incumbents, internet-based interference in elections, and a mismatch of resources between the public and the powerful insiders who exercise influence on government lead to government actions that diverge from the ideal described in the ideal theory of democracy. These features of the institutions of democracy are joined by the phenomenon of citizen disaffection, produced by declining economic opportunities and the rise of populist parties with an interest in creating an environment of division and hostility. The institutions and realities of representative electoral democracy represent important aspects of the ontology of government.

Keywords Democracy · Electoral institutions · Influence · Populism · Public choice

In a democracy we expect that the priorities and policies adopted by government should correspond to the preferences of the citizens. Representative democracy is not a form of direct democracy, where collective decision-making derives from direct polling of the electorate on policy issues. In representative democracies citizens normally are empowered only to express their preferences through their ability to elect officials to offices as legislators and chief executives. When legislators adopt laws to which many citizens object, citizens' primary recourse is to elect different legislators pledged to a different set of priorities and values. Knowing this, elected officials have a strong interest in supporting legislation and policy that conform to the priorities held by a majority of the voters in their districts. Electoral competition is therefore an important ontological fact within a modern democracy: legislators adjust the priorities on the basis of which they decide to support or oppose proposed legislation based in part on their estimation of the likely effect their decision will have on the approval of their constituents. Elected and appointed officials are subject to influence by powerful outsiders, through promises of financial support, self-serving arguments about the supposed benefits of their industry to the common good, and threats of negative actions if their positions are not supported. As we will see below, factors like these make the conduct of government a contested process. The institutions and realities of representative electoral democracy represent important aspects of the ontology of government.

In addition to the aggregation of individual preferences for candidates, democratic theory must consider the circumstances under which the members of a group form their beliefs and preferences. Narrow democratic theory takes individual preferences as exogenous. But broader versions of democratic theory attempt to bring democratic values into the social processes through which beliefs and preferences are formed. The theory of *deliberative democracy* emphasizes in particular the features of civility, mutual respect, and open-mindedness through which debate and critical examination of issues leads to a fuller understanding of issues and a more reflective set of preferences (Gutmann and Thompson 2004; Fung and Wright 2003). This aspect of democracy is valuable because it corresponds to a society in which open debate leads to the formation of individual and collective preferences and embodies the ideas of democratic equality among citizens. And less-advantaged groups can exercise their voices in these forums to attempt to influence other citizens to support more just policies and choices.

Regrettably much of the recent experience in Western democracies undermines confidence in the idea that today's democratic societies are creating an environment in which rational debate and opinions can change; instead, we see the proliferation of internet-driven meme machines that influence micro-targeted segments of the electorate (McAdam and Kloos 2014). The vitriol on the media and Internet outlets sets a tone that discourages or extinguishes respectful debate and clarification. It is hard to see evidence that voters have gotten better at thinking through the issues, the facts, and the underlying values that can subsequently guide their political choices in the ways advocated by the theory of deliberative democracy.

The political power of the electorate is offset, of course, by the political power and influence wielded by elite minorities. Corporations and wealthy individuals are able to influence legislation, regulation, and policy in ways that are vastly disproportionate to their numbers. It is *possible* for a numerous group to exert political influence through the electoral process to defend its interests; but it is also possible for the powerful to quietly subvert these outcomes as well (Culpepper 2010). An alien political scientist might be tempted to classify British, French, or US democracies as a different kind of political institution, a "constitutionally regulated oligarchy with periodic elections of government officials and extensive infrastructures for managing elections to lead to outcomes that satisfy the economically and politically powerful".

Plainly there are property-based influences within a democracy that permit some individuals and groups to wield disproportionate influence in politics. What countervailing factors exist that can help to secure political equality in a contemporary democracy? There seem to be several.

- First, an independent press can serve as a check on anti-democratic and corrupt usurpation of the democratic process.
- Second, a broadly shared public commitment to constitutional procedures can help to reduce the likelihood of anti-democratic seizure of power, whether by leaders or other powerful social forces.
- Third, a well-developed, stable, and secure civil and military bureaucracy can serve as a bulwark against the misuse of power by political leaders.
- Fourth, a strong ethical conviction among civil servants and the military of the priority of constitutionality can reduce the likelihood of unconstitutional steps by government or military.

- Fifth, a tradition of a neutral and independent judiciary can constrain the emergence of anti-democratic leaders.
- Finally, and most important, citizens can remain vigilant and courageous in the face of corruption and anti-democratic actions by government, legislators, and power-holders. Citizens can return to the streets when their government deviates from constitutionality and democracy.

A Pragmatist Theory of Democracy

Jack Knight and Jim Johnson (2012) propose to consider democracies as real existing social systems embodying particular instances of various kinds of institutions. They want to know how those institutions are likely to emerge, and they want to know how they function in real social settings. Here is how they describe the tasks of political theory: "The first analytical task requires that we identify the set of feasible social institutions, examine their respective features, and delineate the conditions necessary for the effective operation of different members of the set" (Knight and Johnson 2012: 13). The second task is explanatory: to account for how specific alternatives emerged over others to become the preponderant institutions in a given society. The third task is normative: to show how we can compare alternative institutions in terms of their contribution to the social good.

Knight and Johnson offer a succinct description of the situation of politics: diversity across a population and conflicts of interest within the population. Citizens disagree, and political institutions serve to reconcile disagreement. The challenge of politics is to create institutions that permit decision-making for a whole society in light of this irreducible diversity, and avoiding dictatorship and violence in the process.

So what is *pragmatist* about the theory of democracy they offer? One feature is straightforward; their work owes a great deal to John Dewey's ideas about democracy. Dewey believed that democracy should be justified on the pragmatic grounds that it created ways of resolving conflicts that were less costly than violence and coercion. More fundamentally, a pragmatist justification for democracy is one that attempts to show that the effects of democratic institutions are overall better for society than those of any of the alternatives. "Pragmatists assess the value of their choices and actions in terms of the consequences of those choices and actions" (Knight and Johnson 2012: 194). So the justification of an institution derives from its overall effectiveness (in conjunction with other institutions) in securing desirable outcomes.

Another aspect of the authors' association with the philosophy of pragmatism has to do with the anti-foundationalism that is associated with pragmatism. Political theory cannot work on the assumption that there is a final truth about political institutions; rather, arguments and conclusions are fallible and contestable. But a steady point of reference is an assessment of how the institutions that a political philosophy advocates will actually work for the population governed by those institutions. We test the recipe by tasting the pudding.

Knight and Johnson refer to a handful of types of institutions that seem to hang together in terms of the idea of governing and managing conflicts over resources and power in a modern society (Knight and Johnson 2012: 7ff.). They refer to economic exchange (markets), distribution of the franchise, constitutional politics, democratic decision-making, and security of property rights and common pool resources. These conditions establish a minimum set of standards for democratic equality and participation; when secured they make it possible for political solutions to conflicts to emerge that are acceptable to all parties. As they point out, each of these families of institutions encompasses a wide range of institutional alternatives; in fact, the constant fact of institutional diversity is one of their persistent themes. A realized democratic society is one that has developed specific institutional arrangements in each of these areas. It is their central argument that democratic institutions need to have *priority* in the process of choosing other institutional arrangements.

In particular, when Knight and Johnson argue for the priority of democracy, they are centrally concerned to show that democratic institutions have priority over market institutions. They concede that there are many tasks where decentralized markets are more efficient ways of handling social and economic conflicts; but they argue that we are nonetheless better off overall to give priority to the institutions of democratic decision-making. Democracy protects the equal voice of all citizens in collective decisions, and markets do not.

Remaining Divided

Knight and Johnson deliberately avoid idealizing democratic theory; they recognize that conflict between individuals and groups over important issues are inherent in social life. That said, the experience of democracy in the past fifty years has been remarkably divisive, and these divisions have all too often emerged along racial and ethnic lines. Why is part of the American electoral system so susceptible to conservative populist appeals, often highlighting themes of racism and intergroup hostility? Doug McAdam and Karina Kloos (2014) address the causes of the radical swing to the right of the Republican Party in *Deeply Divided: Racial Politics and Social Movements in Postwar America*. They believe that the answer lies in the political advantage accruing to focused and dedicated social movements over the majority of the electorate.

McAdam and Kloos argue that social movements are commonly relevant to electoral and party politics. They suggest that the period of relatively high consensus around the moderate middle of the electorate (1940s and 1950s) was exceptional precisely because of the absence of powerful social movements during these decades. But during more typical periods, national electoral politics are influenced by both political parties *and* social movements; and the dynamics of the latter can have complex effects on the behavior and orientation of the former. McAdam and Kloos argue that the social movements associated with the 1960s Civil Rights movement and its opposite, the white segregationist movement, put in motion a political dynamic that pushed each party away from its "median voter" platform, with the Republican Party moving increasingly in the direction of white supremacy and preservation of white privilege. They believe that the dynamics of grassroots social movements help to explain how positions that were unpalatable to the broad electorate nonetheless became committed platforms within the parties. The primary voting processes adopted by the parties after the 1968 Democratic convention gave a powerful advantage to highly committed social activists, even if they do not represent the majority of a party's members.

This historical analysis gives an indication of an even more basic political factor in American politics: the polarizing forces that surround race and the struggle for racial equality. The Civil Rights movement of the 1950s and 1960s was a widespread mobilization of large numbers of ordinary citizens in support of equal rights for African Americans in terms of voting, residence, occupation, and education. Leaders like Ralph Abernathy, Julian Bond, or Martin Luther King, Jr. and organizations like the NAACP, the Congress of Racial Equality, and the Student Nonviolent Coordinating Committee were effective in their call to action for ordinary people to take visible actions to support greater equality through legal means. This movement had some success in pushing the Democratic Party towards greater advocacy of reforms promoting racial justice. However, the political backlash against the Democratic Party following the enactment of civil rights legislation spawned its own grassroots mobilizations of people and associations who objected to these forms of racial progress.

But the account offered by McAdam and Kloos suggests a more complicated causal story of the evolution of American electoral politics as well. McAdam and Kloos make the point that the dynamics of party competition by themselves do not suffice to explain the evolution of US politics to the right, towards a more and more polarized relationship between a divided electorate. They show that social movements of varying stripes played a key causal role in shaping party politics themselves. So explaining American electoral politics requires analysis of both parties and movements. But they also inadvertently make another point as well: that there are underlying structural features of American political psychology that explain much of the dynamics of *both* movements and parties, and these are the facts of racial division and the increasingly steep inequalities of income and wealth that divide Americans. So widespread structural and cultural facts about race and class in American society play a very important role in explaining the movements and alliances that have led us to our current situation. To put the point more simply: we are divided politically because we are divided structurally by inequalities of access, property, opportunity, and outcome along lines of race; and the mechanisms of electoral politics are mobilized to challenge and defend the systems that maintain these inequalities.

Defects in Democracy

There are well known defects in the ways that real democracies work, leading to discrepancies between public preferences and policy outcomes. In the United States, for example, we find:

- Gerrymandered Congressional districts that favor the ascendant party in a state legislature
- Organized efforts to suppress voting by poor and minority voters
- Over-representation of rural voters in the composition of the Senate (Utah has as many senators as California)
- The vast influence of corporate and private money in shaping elections and public attitudes
- An electoral-college system that easily permits the candidate winning fewer votes to nonetheless win the Presidency.

It is evident that the system of electoral democracy institutionalized in the United States is far from a neutral, formal system conveying citizen preferences onto outcomes in a fair and equal way. The rules as well as the choices are objects of contention.

But to understand the ascendancy of the conservative right in US politics we need to go beyond these defects. We need to understand the processes through which citizens acquire their political attitudes—thereby explaining their likelihood of mobilization for one party or candidate or another. And we need to understand the mechanisms through which elected representatives are pushed to the extreme positions that are favored by only a minority of their own supporters.

First, what are the mechanisms that lead to the formation of political attitudes and beliefs in individual citizens? That is, of course, a huge question. People have religious values, civic values, family values, personal aspirations, bits of historical knowledge, and so on, all of which come into play in a wide range of settings through personal development. And all of these value tags may serve as a basis for mobilization by candidates and parties. That is the rationale for "dog-whistle" politics—to craft messages that resonate with small groups of voters without being noticed by larger groups with different values. So let's narrow it a bit: what mechanisms exist through which activist organizations and leaders can promote specific divisive beliefs and attitudes within a population with a range of existing attitudes, beliefs, and values? In particular, how can conservative populist organizations and parties increase the appeal of their programs of intolerance to voters who are not otherwise pre-disposed to the extremes of populism?

Here the potency of appeals to division, intolerance, and hate is of particular relevance. Populism has almost always depended on a simplistic division between "us" and "them" (Mudde and Kaltwasser 2017; Mudde

2019). The rhetoric and themes of nationalism and racism represent powerful tools in the arsenal of populist mobilization, preying upon suspicion, resentment, and mistrust of "others" in order to gain adherents to a party that promises to take advantages away from those others. The right-wing media play an enormous role in promulgating these messages of division and intolerance in many countries. And the experience of having been left out of a fair share of economic advantages leaves some segments of the population particularly vulnerable to these kinds of appeals. Finally, the under-currents of racism and prejudice are of continuing importance in the political and social identities of many citizens—again leaving them vulnerable to appeals that cater to these prejudices.

Let's next consider the institutional mechanisms through which activist advocacy can be turned into disproportionate effects in legislation. Suppose Representative Smith has been elected on the Republican ticket in a close contest over his Democrat opponent with 51% of the vote. And suppose his constituency includes 15% extreme right voters, 20% moderate right voters, and 16% conservative-leaning independents. Why does Smith go on to support the agenda of the far right, who are after all only less than a third of his own supporters in his district? This results from a mechanism that political scientists seem to understand; it involves the dynamics of the primary system. The extreme right is highly activated, while the center is significantly less so. A candidate who moves to the center is in danger of losing his seat in the next primary to a far-right candidate who can depend upon the support of his or her activist base to defeat Smith. So the 15% of extreme-right voters determine the behavior of the representative.

Gerrymandering plays an important role in these dynamics as well. Smith doesn't have to moderate his policy choices out of concern that he will lose the general election to a more moderate Democrat, because the Republican legislature in his state has ensured that this is a safe seat for the candidate chosen by the party.

In 1991 political scientist Sam Popkin published a short book called *The Reasoning Voter: Communication and Persuasion in Presidential Campaigns*. The title captures Popkin's central hypothesis: that voters make choices on the basis of rational assessment of available evidence. What he adds to this old theory of democratic behavior is the proviso that often the principle of reasoning in question is what he calls "low-information rationality". Unlike traditional rational-choice theories of political behavior, Popkin proposes to make use of empirical results from cognitive psychology—insights into how real people make practical decisions of importance. It is striking how much the environment of political behavior has changed since Popkin's reflections in the 1980s and 1990s. Popkin writes, "Most Americans watch some network television news and scan newspapers several times every week" (25). In the current environment, many voters are primarily influenced by the ideological television network of their choice and the strident voices on social media whom they follow. Moreover, a high percentage of the electorate gets its news from social media outlets rather than formal news organizations. The gist is pretty clear: populism is not primarily about rational consideration of costs and benefits, but rather the political emotions of mistrust, intolerance, and fear.

Disaffected Voters

In *The New Minority: White Working Class Politics in an Age of Immigration and Inequality* Justin Gest (2016) attempts to explain how this movement has been able to draw support from white working class men and women—often in support of policies that are objectively harmful to them. Here is how he describes his central concern: "In this book, I suggest that these trends [towards polarization] intensify an underlying demographic phenomenon: the communities of white working class people who once occupied the political middle have decreased in size and moved to the fringes, and American and European societies are scrambling to recalibrate how they might rebuild the centrist coalitions that engender progress" (viii). The book makes use of both ethnographic and survey research to attempt to understand the political psychology of these populations of men and women in Western Europe and the United States—low-skilled workers with limited education beyond secondary school, and with shrinking opportunities in the economies of the 2000s.

A particularly interesting feature of the book is the ethnographic attempt Gest makes to understand the mechanisms and content of this migration of political identity. Gest conducted open-ended interviews with working class men and women in East London and Youngstown, Ohio in the United States—both cities that were devastated by the loss of industrial jobs and the weakening of the social safety net in the 1970s and 1980s. He calls these "post-traumatic cities" (Gest 2016: 7). He addresses the fact that white working class people in those cities and elsewhere now portray themselves as a disadvantaged minority.

The political psychology of resentment plays a large role in the populations he studies—resentment of government that fails to deliver, resentment of immigrants, resentment of affirmative action for racial minorities. The other large idea that Gest turns to is *marginality*—the idea that these groups have that their voices will not be heard and that the powerful agents in society do not care about their fates. And resentment and marginality lead for some individuals to a political stance of resistance. The resentments and expressions of marginality in Youngstown are similar, with an added measure of mistrust of large corporations like the steel companies that abandoned the city and a recognition of the pervasive corruption that permeates the city.

The overriding impression gained from these interviews and Gest's narrative is one of hopelessness. These men and women of Youngstown don't seem to see any way out for themselves or their children. The pathway of upward mobility through post-secondary education does not come up at all in these conversations. And, as Case and Deaton argue from US mortality statistics (2017), social despair is associated with life-ending behaviors such as opioids, alcohol abuse, and suicide.

Gest's book lays the ground for thinking about a post-traumatic democratic politics—a politics that is capable of drawing together the segments of American or British society who genuinely need progressive change and more egalitarian policies if they are to benefit from economic progress in the future. But given the cultural and political realities that Gest identifies among this "new minority", it is hard to avoid the conclusion that crafting such a political platform will be challenging.

Yascha Mounk (2018) considers many of these challenges to democracy and raises considerable anxiety about possible challenges to liberal democracy. He is especially concerned about the authoritarian tendencies that have emerged out of populist politics in numerous western democracies. "The fear that populist insurgents would undermine liberal institutions if they came to power may sound alarmist. But it is based on plenty of precedent. After all, illiberal populists have already been elected to office in countries like Poland and Turkey. In each of these places, they took strikingly similar steps to consolidate their power: they ratcheted up tensions with perceived enemies at home and abroad; packed courts and electoral commissions with their cronies; and took control of the media.... The rise of illiberal democracy, or democracy without rights, is but one side of politics in the first decades of the twenty-first century. For even as ordinary people have grown skeptical of liberal practices and institutions, political elites have tried to insulate themselves from their anger" (Mounk 2018: 6–8). His central advice is surely correct: maintaining a respectful and inclusive democracy will require positive efforts by citizens and leaders to emphasize the basis of solidarity rather than division that underlies their political institutions (17).

Ontological Implications

This brief consideration of the institutions, dynamics, and current behavior of electoral competition in contemporary democracies raises several important issues concerning the ontology of government. First is the causal role of party politics in the behavior of democratic governments. The personnel of government and their incentives in office are often profoundly conditioned by their assessment of the "mood" of their constituents. Second, the institutions of elections are themselves ontologically relevant to the workings of government. The "big data" technologies that have permitted extreme forms of gerrymandering of electoral districts have had a substantial impact on political outcomes. Third, it is clear that more attention needs to be paid within democratic political theory to political psychology. Thin theories of the voter, motivated by pocketbook issues, no longer seem adequate in an era in which the political emotions of hatred, suspicion, resentment, and division appear so prominent. Fourth, public opinion is radically dependent upon the content and form of the media, both old and new. "Weaponized" uses of social media have proven remarkably potent in influencing elections. Finally, the persistent availability of the techniques of social movements within modern democracies creates potentially unpredictable dynamics of change in those democracies. The Civil Rights movement, the Tea Party movement, and the Marriage Equality movement all demonstrate that the institutions and actions of government can be disrupted by activists and their organizations.

References

Case, Anne, and Angus Deaton. *Mortality and Morbidity in the 21st Century*. Brookings Papers on Economic Activity, Spring, 2017.
Culpepper, Pepper. *Quiet Politics and Business Power: Corporate Control in Europe and Japan*. Cambridge; New York: Cambridge University Press, 2010.

Fung, Archon, and Erik Olin Wright. *Deepening Democracy: Institutional Innovations in Empowered Participatory Governance.* The Real Utopias Project 4. London: Verso, 2003.
Gest, Justin. *The New Minority: White Working Class Politics in an Age of Immigration and Inequality.* Oxford; New York: Oxford University Press, 2016.
Gutmann, Amy, and Dennis Thompson. *Why Deliberative Democracy?* Princeton, NJ: Princeton University Press, 2004.
Knight, Jack, and Jim Johnson. *The Priority of Democracy: Political Consequences of Pragmatism.* Princeton, NJ: Princeton University Press, 2012.
McAdam, Doug, and Karina Kloos. *Deeply Divided: Racial Politics and Social Movements in Postwar America.* Oxford; New York: Oxford University Press, 2014.
Mounk, Yascha. *The People vs. Democracy: Why Our Freedom Is in Danger and How to Save It.* Cambridge: Harvard University Press, 2018.
Mudde, Cas. *The Far Right Today.* Cambridge, UK; Malden, MA: Polity, 2019.
Mudde, Cas, and Cristobal Rovira Kaltwasser. *Populism: A Very Short Introduction.* 2nd ed. Oxford; New York: Oxford University Press, 2017.

CHAPTER 8

What Does Government Do?

Abstract This chapter provides a treatment of what government *does*. It is common to speak of government as if it has intentions, beliefs, plans, and fears. However, government is an extended network of offices, bureaus, departments, analysts, decision-makers, and authority structures, each of which has extensive internal structure. This implies the likelihood of a lack of coherence in the intentions and actions of government. Chief executives at a range of levels often have the aspiration of directing the organization as a tightly unified and purposive unit. However, it is plain that the behaviors of functional units within organizations are only loosely controlled by the will of the executive. This ontological fact makes the strategic action field model of organizations directly pertinent to understanding the processes and dynamics of government. The chapter argues that we must also take into account the influence of powerful outsiders on legislation and policy formation. The chapter also considers the role that scientific expertise plays within government policy creation, and identifies some of the sources of pressure and distortion to which scientific experts are subject in policy development.

Keywords Agencies · Environmental Policy · Executives · Knowledge creation · Policy creation · Policy implementation · Science policy

In these final chapters we turn to a treatment of what government *does*, and the social realities that embody and constrain the nature of government thinking and action. We often speak of government as if it has intentions, beliefs, plans, and fears. This sounds a lot like a mind. But this impression is fundamentally misleading. "Government" is not a conscious entity with a unified apperception of the world and its own intentions. Government is not one unified thing. Rather, it is an extended network of offices, bureaus, departments, analysts, decision-makers, and authority structures, each of which has its own reticulated internal structure. This unavoidably implies a likelihood of a lack of coherence in the "mentality" of government.

This has an important consequence. Instead of asking "what is the policy of the United States government towards Africa?", we are often driven to ask subordinate questions: what are the policies towards Africa of the State Department, the Department of Defense, the Department of Commerce, the Central Intelligence Agency, or the Agency for International Development? Further, for each of these departments we are forced to recognize that each is itself a large bureaucracy, with sub-units that have chosen or adapted their own working policy objectives and priorities. There are chief executives at a range of levels—President of the United States, Secretary of State, Secretary of Defense, Director of CIA—and each often has the aspiration of directing his or her organization as a tightly unified and purposive unit. But it is perfectly plain from earlier chapters that the behavior of functional units within organizations is only loosely controlled by the will of the executive. This is part of the meaning of the idea that organizations are often loosely coupled (Chapter 6). This does not mean that executives have no control over the activities and priorities of subordinate units. But it does reflect a simple and unavoidable fact about large organizations. Organizations generally show much more internal differences of opinion and day-to-day purposiveness than a simple organization chart would suggest.

This ontological fact about government makes the relevance of the strategic action field model of organizations directly pertinent to understanding the processes and dynamics of government (Chapter 4). Actions and policies that may appear irrational from the point of view of intelligent manifestations of longterm policy and value goals are comprehensible when we understand them as the result of contending actors and factions. Coalitions within and between agencies and executive offices; decision processes that are influenced by powerful outsiders (corporations, industry groups, citizen advocacy groups, political party activists, ...); and self-serving opportunistic behavior by actors at various levels within the organizational hierarchy all point to the likelihood that resultant policy choices will appear incoherent and inconsistent.

What does government do? In brief, government establishes a framework of law and policy within which society functions. Of particular interest is the government function of creating new policies to address perceived problems in society. Governments formulate policies in service of their priorities. A policy is a set of actions designed to bring about a set of social outcomes—increase post-secondary educational attainment, decrease automobile accident fatalities, end child malnutrition. Setting policy therefore unavoidably involves gathering data about the processes in question and arriving at estimates of the effects various possible interventions are likely to have. Policies, the action plans of government, may be the result of legislation or executive action through the workings of various governmental agencies, and both types of processes raise interesting issues. The implementation of policy requires the ability of government to secure appropriate behavior by citizens, businesses, and government officials alike; this challenge is the topic of Chapter 9 where we consider how government exerts its will.

Consider a few familiar examples. The War on Poverty and resulting Economic Opportunity Act (1964) was President Lyndon B. Johnson's effort to create processes of social and economic change that would end severe poverty in the United States. The Civil Rights Act (1964) and the Voting Rights Act (1965) were aimed at eliminating racial discrimination in public and social life in the United States. The environmental legislation of the 1960s and 1970s was aimed at halting and reversing the decline of environmental quality witnessed in mid-twentieth-century in the United States and the adverse effects on public health and quality of life that ensued. President Bill Clinton's effort at reforming the Federal welfare system resulted in The Personal Responsibility and Work Opportunity Act of 1996, a body of legislation intended to address what conservative critics perceived to be abuses of the existing system of social assistance. Decades-long efforts to reform the way that healthcare insurance is provided to Americans eventually led to passage of the Obama administration's Affordable Care Act (2010)—with years of subsequent efforts by political actors in the opposition party to undo the policy. In each case there was a perceived social or political problem; a process conducted through agencies and executive working groups aimed at developing a policy proposal; a legislative process through which the policy is adopted; and implementation and enforcement of the requirements of the new laws.

Every step of this schematic process of policy creation raises aggregation problems of the kinds described in previous chapters. How do advocates for solutions to perceived social problems gain influence, and how do they come to prevail in official policy-making circles? How are possible policy solutions developed, and what factors determine which solution will gain primacy within the governmental process? What kinds of political coalitions and external influences shape the legislative process through which a policy framework is turned into legislation? Finally, what obstacles arise within government and between government and society when it comes to implementation and enforcement of new policy legislation?

It is apparent that there is a great deal of contingency in each step of this process. Different problems could have been selected, or different formulations of the chosen problems could have been developed; different policy solutions could have been developed; for a given policy framework advocated by a powerful policy stakeholder (the President, for example), different legislative embodiments could have been crafted with very different operational characteristics; and implementation and enforcement depend on the decisions made at a range of governmental levels about priorities, resources, and effort concerning operationalization of the legislation.

Take healthcare reform as an example. The reforms that the Obama administration fought for were plainly advantageous for a very large segment of the American population. Tens of millions of people stood to gain access to health insurance as a consequence of the reforms. Barbara Ehrenreich (2001) makes very clear the importance of healthcare for poor people in her close studies of low-income life experiences. And yet the voices of those tens of millions of uninsured low-income people played almost no role in the bitter political conflict that ensued. Moreover, the Obama plan was certainly not radical or progressive; as Norm Ornstein (2015) observed, the details of the Obama plan derived from a long line of Republican proposals deriving from former Republic Governor of Massachusetts Mitt Romney and Republican Senators Chafee, Durenberger, Grassley, and Hatch. However, Republican opposition to "Obamacare" was unrelenting in the House and the Senate. Conservative theories and agendas, concerted efforts by conservative think-tanks, widely disseminated falsehoods ("death panels"), and heated rhetoric instead dominated the legislative and electoral process. Eventually a weakened version of healthcare reform became law in the form of the Affordable Care Act, on the strength of straight party-line votes in both the House and the Senate. Since passage, key provisions of the legislation were reversed by the Supreme Court and the next presidential administration.

How can we attempt to understand the development, articulation, and legislation surrounding a major piece of policy legislation? It is useful to address these processes from both a micro- and a macro-level of analysis. At the micro-level, we can look closely at the factors that played a role in each stage of the process—the political calculations of the participants, the processes of policy analysis through which experts attempted to assess the probable consequences of various policy options, and the intra-governmental processes through which the policy progressed from political rhetoric to law. This is the level of analysis for which the kinds of mechanisms described in the preceding chapters are most pertinent.

We can also look at the question from the macro point of view: what kinds of macro-level factors influenced the formulation and adoption of a given government policy? Here the kinds of factors that are relevant include the broad environmental characteristics of the field within which policy-makers and elected officials function. These include political ideology, social movements (the Tea Party movement, for example), shifts in public opinion (the abrupt upward shift in acceptance of single-sex marriage that occurred in the 2000s in the United States, for example), and broad economic circumstances during a period of time (affluence, growth, recession, unemployment). International factors are also pertinent; for example, McAdam (1999) argues that the ideological competition associated with the Cold War was a critical factor in the success of civil rights legislation in the mid-1960s. Factors like these have causal influence through their ability to shift the ways that elected leaders give priority to one kind of problem over another, how officials frame the problems they wish to address, and the political calculations they make about the advantage or disadvantage to themselves and their parties of a given policy initiative. Ideologies (e.g. business-conservative Republicans, pro-labor Democrats, social-issue Republicans, multicultural Democrats) lead candidates and elected officials to think about the world in particular ways. Movements like the Tea Party or Occupy Wall Street create the possibility of political damage to the elected official for making the "wrong" choice on a given issue. Economic anxiety among voters may give elected officials more reason to exercise caution in their policy formulations (for example, favoring economic and business growth over control of greenhouse gases and climate change).

Culture too is a macro-level factor that influences government policy. Sociologist Frank Dobbin (1994) emphasizes the importance of cognitive and cultural frameworks in the adoption of national policy choices in his treatment of the emergence of railroad policy in different countries. He argues that there are significantly different cultures of political and industrial policy in different countries that lead to substantial differences in the ways in which government formulates social and economic policies. "Each Western nation-state developed a distinct strategy for governing industry" (Dobbin 1994: 1). For example, the *laissez-faire* culture of the United States permitted a few large railroad magnates and corporations to make the crucial decisions about technology, standards, and routes that would govern the development of the rail system. The regulated market culture of Great Britain favored smaller companies and strove to prevent the emergence of a small number of oligopolistic rail companies. And the technocratic civil-service culture of France gave a great deal of power to the engineers and civil servants who were charged to make decisions about technology choice, routes, and standards. Dobbin's work demonstrates the very great degree of contingency that exists in the implementation of public policy. Second, it makes a strong case for the idea that an element of culture—the framework of assumptions, precedents, and institutions defining the "policy culture" of a country—can have a very strong effect on the development of large policies and institutions. Dobbin emphasizes the role that things like traditions, customs, and legacies play in the unfolding of important historical developments. And finally, the work makes it clear that these highly contingent pathways of development nonetheless admit of explanation.

Executive Leadership

Executives attempt to limit the degree of disunity that exists within their span, and this applies to elected presidents, appointed secretaries and directors of major agencies, as well as CEOs of private companies. Shirley Ann Warshaw (1997) makes the case that US presidents since World War II have sought to exert greater control and direction over domestic policy, with mixed results. She writes, "It is the goal of this study to establish how recent presidents have used their White House staffs to frame a domestic policy, organize the often disparate parts of the administration in support of that policy, and build the coalitions of support necessary to move that policy forward.... The organizational structures vary from administration to administration as do the size of the units, the political and policy background of its members, and their roles in managing the general domestic policy process" (Warshaw 1997: 1–2).

Warshaw emphasizes some of the central themes of this book, including consent, collaboration, and authority. She highlights the inherent multiplicity of government—different offices, agencies, and executives possessing different interests and priorities—and the need for concerted efforts to "build coalitions of support" in order to gain a degree of coherence and effectiveness in implementing a package of priorities. "Cabinet acceptance of the legitimate authority of the White House staff therefore depends on a White House staff with clearly formed, well-articulated goals and objectives as established by the president, and similarly depends upon a cabinet committed to those goals and objectives" (Warshaw 1997: 12). She emphasizes as well, however, the degree to which disharmony and conflict characterized efforts within the White House in different administrations to pursue a coherent domestic policy. "This ever-changing role of the domestic council has contributed not only to a lack of continuity in domestic policy but often a certain chaos in the domestic policy office as well.... The absence of either a continuing structure or continuing staff in the management of domestic policy has been reflected in severe problems that each administration has faced in framing a domestic agenda and building both legislative and public support for that agenda" (Warshaw 1997: 3). She argues that the later years of the Clinton administration demonstrates a collapse of unity around the priorities of the domestic policy agenda of the president.

POLICY FORMULATION

Much of the work of government is performed by agencies through policies, actions, and administration of relevant conduct by citizens and private organizations and corporations. Governmental agencies have rule-setting powers and powers of enforcement, delegated by Congress to permit them to carry out their assigned missions—the Federal Emergency Management Agency, the Environmental Protection Agency (EPA), the Food and Drug Administration, or the Social Security Administration.

Agencies implement policies under broad enabling legislation enacted by Congress. They are generally large hierarchical organizations incorporating layers of administrators and technical experts, and the eventual content of a new policy is often the highly complex result of myriad different scientific assessments, interests, and voices. The question here is a somewhat limited one: how do the agencies of government arrive at decisions? What is the role of fact-gathering, opinion-writing, and advocacy in the ultimate decision taken by the department?

The actions of government are complex in several ways. The processes within government are themselves complex and worthy of study. Second, it is also the case that there are powerful and interested parties outside of government who have preferences about the shape that policy takes, and these actors find a variety of ways of making their influence felt. Figure 8.1 gives an overall impression of the complexities of these processes. These competing systems of influence create the likelihood that policy formulation will be a turbulent process.

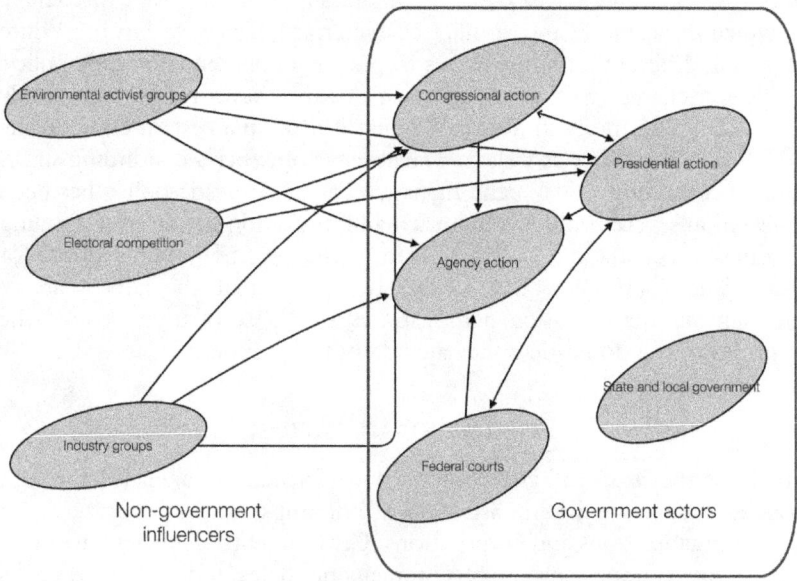

Fig. 8.1 Governmental action (*Source* Author)

Information Gathering and Scientific Assessment

Organizational units at all levels arrive at something analogous to beliefs (assessments of fact and probable future outcomes), assessments of priorities and their interactions, plans, and decisions (actions to take in the near and intermediate future). And governments make decisions at the highest level (leave the EU, raise taxes on fuel, prohibit immigration from certain countries, ...). How does the analytical and factual part of this process proceed? And how does the decision-making part unfold?

Government policy usually requires a factual basis. It is necessary to gather evidence about a problem and to go through a process of evaluating and assessing available data to arrive at a set of beliefs about the problem area. Examples include the risks of nuclear power, the potential toxicity of DDT, the process of global warming, the causes of urban poverty, and the differential racial effects of the War on Drugs. We may look at this as the "cognitive" work of government—the processes through which the organizations and individuals of government arrive at factual beliefs about the policy environment. We need a better understanding of the scientific-bureaucratic processes through which governmental scientific agencies and their committees gather and analyze evidence about the problem. An important causal factor in this area of government activity is the presence of pressure and influence by external stakeholders of many kinds. Industrial groups, corporations, regional interests, and citizen groups all have an interest and an ability to intervene in the policy process. Influence extends throughout the governmental process, from fact gathering and assessment to priority-setting to writing regulations to implementing a regulatory system. Current research in science and technology policy provides an empirically grounded account of the institutional arrangements through which government scientific knowledge and policy are created.

Sometimes governments decide through solitary individuals in a position to do so. The more interesting cases involve situations where there is a genuine collective process through which analysis and assessment takes place (of facts and priorities), and through which policy solutions are considered and ultimately adopted. Agencies usually make decisions through extended and formalized processes. There is generally an organized process of fact gathering and scientific assessment, followed by an assessment of various policy options with public exposure. Finally a policy is adopted (the moment of decision).

It is clear that an important part of the substantial improvement that has occurred in aviation safety in the past fifty years is the effective investigation and reporting provided by the National Transportation Safety Board (NTSB). NTSB is an authoritative and respected bureau of experts whom the public trusts when it comes to discovering the causes of aviation disasters. The Chemical Safety Board (CSB) plays a similar role with regard to the chemical and petrochemical industries. It has a much shorter institutional history—it was created in 1990—but we need to ask a parallel question here as well: Does the CSB provide a strong lever for improving safety practices in the chemical and petrochemical industries through its accident investigations; or are industry actors largely free to continue their poor management practices indefinitely, safe in the realization that large chemical accidents are rare and the costs of occasional liability judgments are manageable?

As Raadschelders and Whetsell (2018) argue, policy decisions are rarely determined by scientific evidence alone. For one thing, scientific experts are sometimes divided in their recommendations; this range of uncertainty is a normal part of scientific practice. But more fundamentally, there is sometimes an unavoidable need for pragmatic balancing of scientific and non-scientific considerations in the decision to establish a given policy, and ethical policy decision-makers need to attempt to achieve such a balance without permitting bias or self-interest to intrude into the outcome. Consider for example the need to establish policies that would resolve the Dakota Access Pipeline conflicts over the route taken by the proposed pipeline. It may be that scientific judgments about the probability of contamination of drinking water by the proposed route are strong and well supported, with the recommendation that the likelihood of contamination is extremely low. Nonetheless a sensible policy-maker may well conclude that the harm created for the public of *fear* of contamination is sufficiently important to justify re-routing the pipeline to avoid that fear. This case would illustrate the need for a balancing of narrow science-based cost-benefit analysis with a broader consideration of the public harms created by anxiety, fear, and discord.

Corporate Assaults on Scientific Research

Science is uncertain; and yet we have no better basis for making important decisions about the future than the best scientific knowledge currently available. However, there are powerful economic interests that exert themselves to undermine the confidence of the public and our policy makers in the findings of science that appear to harm those business interests. How should we think about these two factors, one epistemic and the other political? Naomi Oreskes and Erik Conway (2010) explore the latter dynamics in substantial detail in *Merchants of Doubt*. Oreskes' work on the politics and methods of science denial is substantial and convincing. She is an historian of science, and she has carefully traced the pathways through which business interests have exerted themselves to affect the outcome of a range of scientific debates: for example, the harmful effects of tobacco, acid rain, the reality of an ozone hole, and the reality of global warming. She traces the influence that conservative think tanks and corporations have had on the scientific debates over these issues. But more, she demonstrates that a small number of conservative nuclear scientists have played a key and recurring role in drumming up spurious attacks on the scientific credentials of researchers in a number of these fields.

> Call it the "Tobacco Strategy." Its target was science, and so it relied heavily on scientists— with guidance from industry lawyers and public relations experts— willing to hold the rifle and pull the trigger. Among the multitude of documents we found in writing this book were Bad Science: A Resource Book— a how-to handbook for fact fighters, providing example after example of successful strategies for undermining science, and a list of experts with scientific credentials available to comment on any issue about which a think tank or corporation needed a negative sound bite. (Oreskes and Conway 2010: 6)

The purpose of this strategy was clear to its creators—to create doubt in the minds of citizens and legislators concerning the quality and credentials of the scientific conclusions with which they disagreed. "The industry's position was that there was 'no proof' that tobacco was bad, and they fostered that position by manufacturing a "debate," convincing the mass media that responsible journalists had an obligation to present "both sides" of it. Representatives of the Tobacco Industry Research Committee met with staff at *Time*, *Newsweek*, *U.S. News and World Report*, *BusinessWeek*, *Life*, and *Reader's Digest*, including men and women at the very top of the American media industry" (Oreskes and Conway 2010: 16).

Oreskes and Conway make a very strong case that good scientific research on controversial issues will be drowned out by money and astute public relations strategies by self-interested corporations. And ultimately this possibility has potentially devastating results for public health and our global future, if the public and our policy makers succumb to this attack on science.

Environmental Policy Formation

Here we will consider for the purpose of illustration one part of government's actions, the evolving story of environmental policy in the United States since 1960. This history will serve to illustrate many of the points about social ontology of government that are most important here: legislation, agency action, the role of the public's voice, regulatory regimes, industry efforts to influence government policy, and limitations of the impact of government action in this area.

Richard Nixon was elected president in 1968. A critical step in the evolution of government policy in the area of environmental protection was the establishment of the (EPA) by executive order by President Nixon in December 1970. The EPA was to become the key Federal agency to oversee environmental knowledge-gathering and policy formulation. Various important pieces of legislation have been adopted that give guidance to environmental policy, including the clean air and water acts of the 1960s and 1970s. The formulation of detailed policies and rules to carry out these legislative acts is largely the domain of the staff of the EPA. Figure 8.2 provides a timeline for important events, legislation, and agency action during this time.

How were government policies on environmental issues developed and established as legislation and regulations? How did government *act* during this important period? What were the governmental and social processes through which new environmental policies were considered, adopted, and put into effect? Figure 8.2 gives an idea of the flurry of policies and actions taken by government during this period of several decades, and Table 8.1 provides a list of important pieces of environmental legislation undertaken during this period.

Figure 8.1 gives a very high-level view of the groups of actors inside and outside of government that influenced or created these policies. But Fig. 8.1 presents the situation as a set of black boxes, concealing the complex and intricate pathways of influence, argumentation, and power that played roles in the outcomes of each of the legislative and policy landmarks identified in Fig. 8.2. In order to get a better sense of the intricacy

8 WHAT DOES GOVERNMENT DO? 137

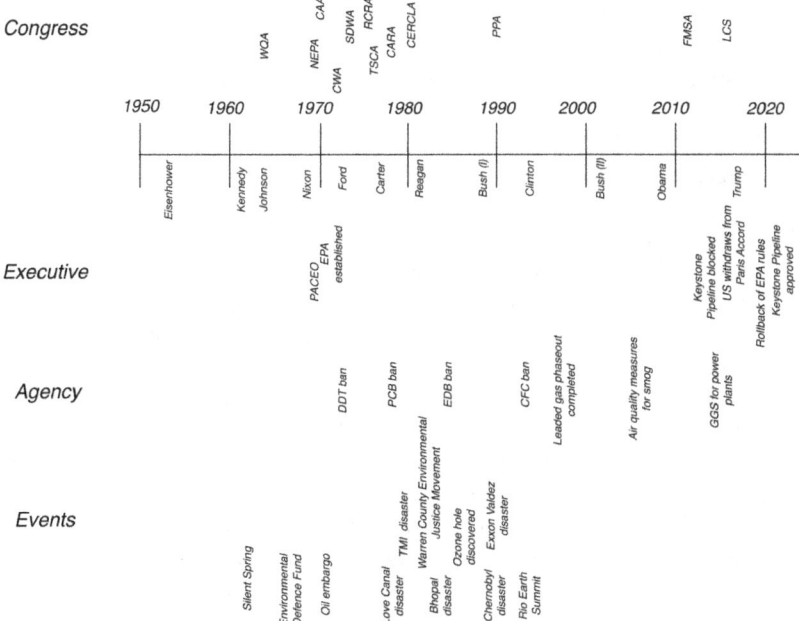

Fig. 8.2 Environmental protection (*Source* Author)

Table 8.1 Environmental legislation

WQA	1965	Water Quality Act
NEPA	1970	National Environmental Policy Act
CAA	1970	Clean Air Act
CWA	1972	Clean Water Act
SDWA	1974	Safe Drinking Water Act
RCRA	1976	Resource Conservation and Recovery Act
TSCA	1976	Toxic Substances Control Act
CARA	1977	Clean Air Act Amendments
CERCLA	1980	Comprehensive Environmental Response, Compensation, and Liability Act
PPA	1990	Pollution Prevention Act
FMSA	2011	Food Modernization and Safety Act
LCS	2016	Lautenberg Chemical Safety for the 21st Century Act

of these internal processes of influence and honest efforts at preserving the health and safety of the public, consider Fig. 8.3, a diagrammatic representation of one important episode of policy creation, the decision to ban DDT in 1972.

The decision by the EPA to ban DDT in 1972 is illustrative. This was a decision of government that eventually became the will of government. It was the result of several important sub-processes: citizen and NGO activism about the possible toxic harms created by DDT, non-governmental scientific research assessing the toxicity of DDT, an internal EPA process designed to assess the scientific conclusions about the environmental and human-health effects of DDT, an analysis of the competing priorities involved in this issue (farming, forestry, and malaria control versus public health), and a decision recommended to the Administrator and adopted that concluded that the priority of public health and environmental safety was weightier than the economic interests served by the use of the pesticide.

The DDT case study sheds important light on the question of the ontology of government. The policy adoption was the result of a messy, bureaucratic, scientific, policy-evaluation, and lobbying process

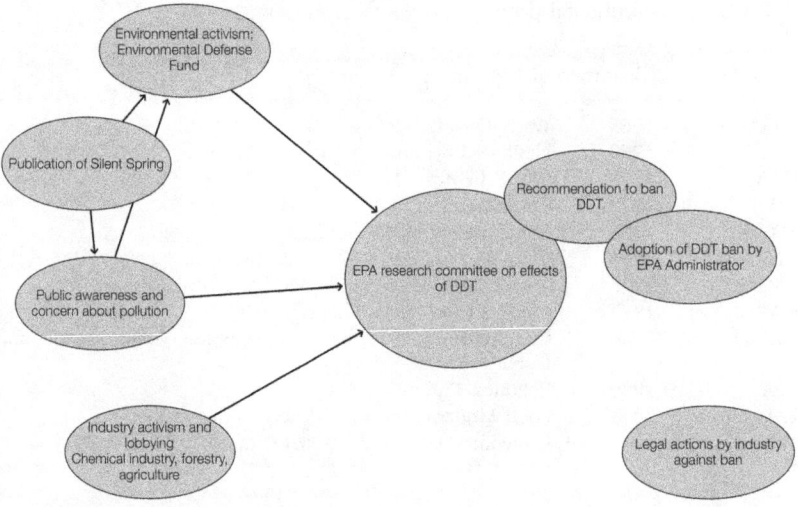

Fig. 8.3 Banning DDT (*Source* Author)

that extended inside the laboratories and policy offices of the EPA, through universities where public health and toxicity experts worked, into the strategic planning of major industries that would be affected by the potential ban. At no point was the process a pure example of rational, scientific factual assessment and policy refinement; instead, there was an intertwining of the economic and political interests of outsiders even as scientific committees within the EPA deliberated about the substance of the issues. Another interesting case is the EPA's risk assessment of passive smoking health effects in 1992 (US EPA 1992). Other examples of agency decision-making concerning science and technology follow a similar pattern.

These cases of the development of science and technology policy illustrate two dimensions of the processes through which a government agency "makes up its mind" about a complex issue. There is an analytical component in which the scientific facts and the policy goals and priorities are gathered and assessed. And there is a decision-making component in which these analytical findings are crafted into a decision—a policy, a set of regulations, or a funding program, for example. It is routine in science and technology policy studies to observe that there is commonly a substantial degree of intertwining between factual judgments and political preferences and influences brought to bear by powerful outsiders.

Ideally we would like to imagine a process of government decision-making that proceeds along these lines: careful gathering and assessment of the best available scientific evidence about an issue through expert specialist panels and sections; careful analysis of the consequences of available policy choices measured against a clear understanding of goals and priorities of the government; and selection of a policy or action that is best, all things considered, for forwarding the public interest and minimizing public harms. Unfortunately, as the experience of government policies concerning climate change in recent years illustrates, ideology and private interest distort every phase of this idealized process.

Processes of Decision-Making

Let us look a bit more closely at the primary mechanisms involved in this account of the formation of national environmental policy. It is common in political science and economics to understand decision-making in terms of a rational process in which the agent appraises his or her preferences, assigns utilities and probabilities to the possible outcomes of each action, and chooses the action that has the greatest expected utility. This is the familiar rational-choice model of decision making, and its close cousin, cost-benefit analysis.

Sociologists and cognitive psychologists alike have made it clear that decision-making is more complicated than this simple model. One of those complications is the set of defects of rationality that were so extensively studied by Kahneman and Tversky (1982) and applied to organizational behavior by Herbert Simon (1997), including different treatment of gains versus losses and over-estimates of high-stakes outcomes. But there are other reasons to believe that decision-making is more complicated and less rational than this simple model would suggest. Every decision-maker brings a set of "framing assumptions" about the reality concerning which he or she is deliberating. These framing assumptions impose an unavoidable kind of cognitive bias into collective decision-making. A business executive brings a worldview to the question of regulation of risk that is quite different from that of an ecologist or an environmental activist. This is different from the point often made about self-interest; our framing assumptions do not feel like expressions of self-interest, but rather simply secure convictions about how the world works and what is important in the world. This is one reason why the work of social scientists like Scott Page (2007) on the value of diversity in problem-solving and decision-making is so important: by bringing multiple perspectives and cognitive frames to a problem, we are more likely to get a balanced decision that gives appropriate weight to the legitimate interests and concerns of all involved.

Here is a concrete illustration of cognitive bias (with a measure of self-interest as well) in Stever's (1980) excellent discussion of siting decisions for nuclear power plants:

> From the time a utility makes the critical in-house decision to choose a site, any further study of alternatives is necessarily negative in approach. Once sufficient corporate assets have been sunk into the chosen site to produce data adequate for state site review, the company's management has a large enough stake in it to resist suggestions that a full study of site alternatives be undertaken as a part of the state (or for that matter as a part of the NEPA) review process. hence, the company's methodological approach to evaluating alternates to the chosen site will always be oriented toward the desired conclusion that the chosen site is superior. (Stever 1980: 30)

Stever's central point here is a very important one: the pace of site selection favors the energy company's choices over the concerns or preferences of affected groups because the company is in a position to have dedicated substantial resources to development of the preferred site proposal. But here is a crucial thing to observe: the siting decision is only one of dozens in the development of a new power plant, which is itself only one of hundreds of government and business decisions made every year. What Stever describes is a structural bias in the regulatory process, not a one-off flaw. At its bottom, this is the task that government faces when considering the creation of a new nuclear power plant: "to assess the various public and private costs and benefits of a site proposed by a utility" (32); and Stever's analysis makes it doubtful that existing public processes do this in a consistent and effective way. Stever argues that government needs to have more of a role in site selection, not less: "The kind of social and environmental cost accounting required for a balanced initial assessment of, and development of, alternative sites should be done by a public body acting not as a reviewer of private choices, but as an active planner" (32).

Legislation

Much of the effort by academic political scientists in the field of American politics is expended on the task of understanding the realities of legislative processes. Gaining a majority in favor of a legislative package requires making compromises. There are often regional interests (sunbelt, rustbelt) that create differing elective interests for senators and representatives. Large business interests find their way into the legislative process through lobbying, campaign contributions, and other forms of influence over legislators.

Legislative decision-making within a democratically elected assembly has its own logic—log-rolling, agenda setting, pork-barrel politics, internal rules, the influence of powerful outsiders, and public opinion. The importance of party affiliation in Congress is increasingly large, with a rising ability of the parties to "discipline" their members to maintain unity around issues endorsed by the party (McAdam and Kloos 2014).

We might provide an abstract description of the legislator by placing him or her in a field of influence involving constituents, political party, business interests, and ideology. An earlier generation of political scientists sought to understand elected officials' electoral calculations in terms of "median voter" theory—the idea that the most popular position will be the position at the center of the preferences of all voters in the district. But, as McAdam and Kloos (2014) and many others have demonstrated, the logic of contested primary elections has polarized electoral competition, leading to results quite different from those predicted by median-voter theory.

The role of Congressional staff is also important in the legislative process. Staff bring areas of expertise to the elected official whom they serve, and they often bring their own convictions about the direction and purpose that legislation should take in a particular issue area. (An extensive scholarly treatment of the role of staff in policy and legislation is provided in Hagedorn [2015]).

Powerful Outsiders

There are also important non-electoral actors whose interests are affected by legislation, including businesses and other economic interests. Business has substantial influence in government (Culpepper 2010). Corporations have strong financial interests in taxation, health and safety regulation, export legislation and policy, and a host of other issues affected by government policy. And they are able to express their interests through lobbying efforts, candidate campaign funds, and personal interventions with powerful government officials. Over $3 billion have been expended annually in federal lobbying efforts in the past several years, with $3.42 billion expended in 2018. Moreover, corporations and industry groups are able to wield influence disproportionate to their size through the concentrated expertise (legal, scientific, technical) that they can bring to the case they make to the government agencies that regulate them.

Pepper Culpepper unpacks the political advantage residing with business elites and managers in terms of acknowledged expertise about the intricacies of corporate organization, an ability to frame the issues for policy makers and journalists, and ready access to rule-writing committees and task forces. These factors give elite business managers positional advantage, from which they can exert a great deal of influence on how an issue is formulated when it comes into the forum of public policy formation. Culpepper refers to British Cadbury Committee, tasked to develop "best practices" in corporate governance (9), as an important example of an occasion where high-level managers had a very powerful ability to write the rules that would govern their behavior. Vice President Cheney's energy committee during the Bush administration is another example. Informal working groups, containing a significant representation of managerial elites, have an ability to set the agenda for a regulatory regime that allows them to privilege positions they prefer and to protect their organizations from worst-case outcomes.

Consider the largest issues we face today in national politics—climate policy, cap-and-trade policy, healthcare reform, and the nation's food system. The influence of large financial interests in each of these areas is visible. Energy companies, coal companies, insurance companies and trade associations, pharmaceutical companies, and large food companies and restaurant chains pretty much run the show. Regulations are written in deference to their interests, legislation conforms to their needs and demands, and elected officials calculate their actions to the winds of campaign contributions. And in 2010 the Supreme Court reversed a century of precedent in its Citizens United v. FEC decision and accorded the rights of freedom of expression to corporations and unions that are enjoyed by individual citizens. As a result the influence of financially powerful corporations and industry groups has become even greater.

References

Culpepper, Pepper. *Quiet Politics and Business Power: Corporate Control in Europe and Japan*. Cambridge ; New York: Cambridge University Press, 2010.

Dobbin, Frank. *Forging Industrial Policy: The United States, Britain, and France in the Railway Age*. Cambridge, UK; New York: Cambridge University Press, 1994.

Ehrenreich, Barbara. *Nickel and Dimed: On (Not) Getting by in America*. 1st ed. New York: Metropolitan Books, 2001.

Hagedorn, Sara. "Taking the Lead: Congressional Staffers and Their Role in the Policy Process." PhD dissertation, University of Colorado, 2015.

Kahneman, Daniel, Paul Slovic, and Amos Tversky. *Judgment under Uncertainty: Heuristics and Biases*. Cambridge: Cambridge University Press, 1982.

McAdam, Doug. *Political Process and the Development of Black Insurgency, 1930–1970*. 2nd ed. Chicago: University of Chicago Press, 1999.

McAdam, Doug, and Karina Kloos. *Deeply Divided: Racial Politics and Social Movements in Postwar America*. Oxford; New York: Oxford University Press, 2014.

Oreskes, Naomi, and Erik M. Conway. *Merchants of Doubt: How a Handful of Scientists Obscured the Truth on Issues from Tobacco Smoking to Global Warming*. New York: Bloomsbury Press, 2010.

Ornstein, Norm. "The Real Story of Obamacare's Birth." *The Atlantic*, July 6, 2015.

Page, Scott E. *The Difference: How the Power of Diversity Creates Better Groups, Firms, Schools, and Societies*. Princeton: Princeton University Press, 2007.

Raadschelders, Jos C. N., and Travis A. Whetsell. "Conceptualizing the Landscape of Decision Making for Complex Problem Solving." *International Journal of Public Administration* 41, no. 14 (2018): 1132–44.

Simon, Herbert A. *Administrative Behavior: A Study of Decision-Making Processes in Administrative Organizations*. 4th ed. New York: Free Press, 1997 [1947].

Stever, Donald W. Jr. *Seabrook and the Nuclear Regulatory Commission: The Licensing of a Nuclear Power Plant*. University Press of New England, 1980.

US EPA. *Respiratory Health Effects of Passive Smoking: Lung Cancer and Other Disorders*. EPA/600/6-90/006F. Washington, DC: US EPA Federal Registry, 1992.

Warshaw, Shirley Anne. *The Domestic Presidency: Policy Making in the White House*. Needham Heights, MA: Allyn & Bacon, 1997.

CHAPTER 9

Governments as Regulators

Abstract This chapter turns to the role that government plays in regulating activities that pose risks to public health and safety. How does government establish and implement prudent schemes of regulation of risky activities? Enforcement of regulations and policies faces many of the same obstacles considered in previous chapters: principal-agent problems within government, non-compliance by actors in civil society, and deliberate efforts at evasion of regulation by actors at every scale. To this list we can add the fact of regulatory capture: the ability of corporations and industries to influence legislators and agency officials in favor of less restrictive regulation and enforcement. How does government attempt to secure a sufficiently high level of compliance with rules and regulations in the economic sphere? How effective are private power-holders in influencing the regulatory process and in shaping the enforcement mechanisms considered by regulatory agencies? The chapter considers the system of "delegated regulation" as a government arrangement that is vulnerable to conflict of interest and regulatory capture. The Nuclear Regulatory Commission is taken as a case study.

Keywords Aviation safety · Environmental protection · Nuclear safety · Regulatory capture · Regulatory system

A fundamental problem for understanding the mechanics of government is the question of how the will and intentions of government (policies, rules, tax schemes) are conveyed from the sites of decision-making to the behavior of the actors whom these policies are meant to influence. Once goals and priorities are set and policies are developed, government needs to act. What are the levers through which the will of government is transformed into effective influence on the actions of citizens, organizations, and corporations? Governments intend implement policy goals (ensure the health and safety of the public) and to change behavior of the actors in civil society (taxpayers, polluters, insurance companies, nuclear power plant operators, automobile drivers). Implementation of policies requires the creation of extended plans for action involving multiple agencies of government and partner institutions. Enforcement begins with the formulation of rules and regulations. But enforcement of regulations and policies faces many of the same obstacles considered in previous chapters: principal-agent problems within government, non-compliance by actors in civil society, deliberate efforts at evasion of regulation by actors at every scale. How does government handle the internal problems of consistent implementation by its agents? And how does it attempt to secure a sufficiently high level of compliance with rules and regulations in civil society?

The familiar principal-agent problem designates precisely this complex of issues (Chapter 6). Applying a government policy or regulation requires a chain of behaviors by multiple agents within an extended network of governmental and non-governmental offices. It is all too evident that actors at various levels have interests and intentions that are important to their choices; and blind obedience to commands from above is not a common practice within any organization. Instead, actors within an office or bureau have some degree of freedom to act strategically with regard to their own preferences and interests. What, then, are the arrangements that the principal can put in place that makes conformance by the agent more complete?

Further, there are commonly numerous non-governmental entities and actors who are affected by governmental policies and regulations. They too have the ability to act strategically in consideration of their preferences and interests. And some of the actions that are available to non-governmental actors have the capacity to significantly influence the impact and form of various governmental policies and regulations. The corporations that own nuclear power plants, for example, have an ability to constrain and deflect the inspection schedules to which their properties are subject through influence on legislators, and the regulatory agency may be seriously hampered in its ability to apply existing safety regulations.

This is a problem of social ontology: what kind of thing is a governmental agency, how does it work internally, and through what kinds of mechanisms does it influence the world around it (firms, criminals, citizens, local governments, ...)? The idea of organizations as "strategic action fields" that is developed by Fligstein and McAdam (2012) fits the situation of a governmental agency well, both internally and externally. Coalitions of actors within an organization or government department determine the effectiveness of the organization's ability to formulate and implement its will. And coalitions of actors outside the organization have major impact on the question of whether or not the will of the organization is effectively realized in the broader environment of private and business activity. This latter point is the thrust of the "open-system framework" for understanding the workings of organizations (Chapter 4).

Government Regulation of Industry

Since the beginning of the industrial age the topic of regulation of private activity for the public good has been essential for the health and safety of the public. The economics of externalities and public harms are too powerful to permit private actors to conduct their affairs purely according to the dictates of profit and private interest. The desolation of the River Irk in Manchester described by Friedrich Engels (1958 [1845]) in the 1840s created by reckless factory development was powerful evidence of this dynamic in the nineteenth century, and the need for the protection of health and safety in the food industry, the protection of air and water quality, and establishment of regulations ensuring safe operation of industrial, chemical, and nuclear plants became abundantly evident in the middle of the twentieth century. Major regulators of industry in the United States include the Environmental Protection Agency, the Food and Drug Administration, and the Occupational Safety and Health Administration. Also important are safety agencies such as the Nuclear Regulatory Commission, the National Transportation Safety Board, and the Chemical Safety Board. Their tasks are defined variously, but at bottom, they are all created to ensure the safety and health of the public with regard to a range of potentially harmful private activities.

When we consider of the issues of health and safety that exist in a modern complex economy, it is impossible to imagine that these social goods will be adequately protected by market forces alone. Health and safety hazards are typically regarded as "externalities" by private companies—if they can be "dumped" on the public without cost, this is good for the profitability of the company. It is clear that state regulation is the appropriate remedy for this tendency of a market-based economy to chronically produce hazards and harms, whether in the form of environmental pollution, unsafe foods and drugs, or unsafe industrial processes. But how can a modern regulatory system be designed that will perform its public tasks effectively? Throughout the previous chapters we have seen the pervasiveness of the influence wielded on government decisions and actions by powerful outsiders; so how can a regulatory agency be expected to impose its rules on industry? The situation for regulation is even more challenging in light of the technical complexity and rapid innovation that most industries display. It is difficult for government regulators to have the levels of expertise necessary to evaluate complicated new financial instruments in the financial sector or the risks of new aviation software in the aircraft industry; the expertise and in-depth knowledge needed for these tasks are more often located in the industry rather than the government.

Joseph Stiglitz (2009) presents the task of government regulation in terms of the serious and harmful consequences of market failure. Stiglitz puts the point about market failure very clearly: "Only under certain ideal circumstances may individuals, acting on their own, obtain 'pareto efficient' outcomes, that is, situations in which no one can be made better off without making another worse off. These individuals involved must be rational and well informed, and must operate in competitive marketplaces that encompass a full range of insurance and credit markets. In the absence of these ideal circumstances, there exist government interventions that can potentially increase societal efficiency and/or equity" (Stiglitz 2009: 11). For straightforward economic reasons, regulation is unpopular—with the businesses, landowners, developers, and other powerful agents whose actions are constrained. So how can regulation be effective? Stiglitz pays attention to the pervasive problem of "regulatory capture"—the ability of the regulated industry and corporations to influence or block the regulatory requirements of the agency that has jurisdiction. This ability may come through an ability to lobby legislators or officials of the agency itself for favorable implementation of proposed rules, or through the "revolving door" through which former executives of the industry take decision-making roles within the agency, or it may take the form of an ability to deflect regulatory action altogether through political influence.

It is clear, then, that regulatory systems face substantial obstacles in their mission to ensure the safety of complex and expensive technologies. A critical challenge for regulatory agencies is the role that economic and political power plays in deforming the operations of governmental agencies to serve the interests of the powerful. Regulatory agencies are "captured" by the powerful industries they are supposed to oversee, whether through influence on the executive branch or through incessant and effective lobbying of the legislative branch.

Another key obstacle is the cost, in dollars and expert staff, that would be required for comprehensive regulation, inspection, and oversight of industry. In the United States this problem has been addressed in recent decades through a system of *delegated regulation*, in which much of the detailed work necessary for regulatory oversight is delegated to the experts within the industry or corporation themselves. For example, the Federal Aviation Administration (FAA) delegates more than 90% of the effort required for certifying a new aircraft to the manufacturers, and safety in the petrochemical industry is almost entirely delegated to the corporations and industry producing and refining petrochemical products. OSHA maintains regulatory authority with regard to the health and safety of workers in petrochemical plants, but the hazards of the chemical industry far exceed the risks of injury in the workplace. The Chemical Safety Board is convened only after a major chemical plant accident has occurred, and is empowered only to provide an analysis of the causes of the accident and recommendations for improvements of processes. The Texas City oil refinery fire in 2005 is instructive (Hopkins 2008).

The tragedy of the Boeing 737 MAX of 2018–2019 appears to be a clear recent instance where regulatory oversight failed (Raso 2019). The economic power of large aircraft manufacturers appears to have succeeded in reducing the ability of the FAA to establish processes leading to safe design and operation of this aircraft, including review of the revised autopilot system intended to handle anti-stall emergencies created by the placement of larger engines. Executives and lobbyists exercised their ability to influence powerful senators and members of

Congress through person-to-person interactions. And elected representatives from both parties favored "less regulation" as a way of supporting the economic interests of businesses in their states.

It is apparent that this system of delegation creates the possibility of crippling the regulatory process by placing crucial parts of the evaluation in the hands of experts whose interests and careers lie in the hands of the corporation whose product they are evaluating. This creates an inherent conflict of interest for the employee, and it is potentially a critical flaw in the process from the point of view of safety. Congress has encouraged this program of delegation in order to constrain budget growth for the federal agency.

These kinds of influence on legislation and agency action provide clear illustrations of the mechanisms cited by Pepper Culpepper (2010) explaining the political influence of business. Culpepper unpacks the political advantage residing with business elites and managers in terms of acknowledged expertise about the intricacies of corporate organization, an ability to frame the issues for policy makers and journalists, and ready access to rule-writing committees and task forces. These factors give elite business managers positional advantage, from which they can exert a great deal of influence on how an issue is formulated when it comes into the forum of public policy formation.

It seems clear that the "regulatory delegation" movement in Congress and industry and its underlying effort to reduce regulatory burden on industry has had substantial effect in the field of aviation, and the same seems true in other industries such as the nuclear industry. The much harder question is organizational: what form of regulatory oversight would permit a regulatory industry to genuinely enhance the safety of the regulated industry and protect the public from unnecessary hazards? Even if we could take the anti-regulation ideology that has governed much public discourse since the Reagan years out of the picture, there are the continuing issues of expertise, funding, and industry power of resistance that make effective regulation a huge challenge.

Another culprit in this story of failure of government regulation is the conservative penchant for leaving everything to private enterprise. As Michael Brown put the point during his tenure as director of FEMA during the Katrina Hurricane disaster, "the general idea—that the business of government is not to provide services, but to make sure that they are provided—seems self-evident to me" (quoted in Perrow 2011b: 112). The sustained ideological war against government regulation that has been underway since the Reagan administration has had disastrous consequences when it comes to safety. Activities like nuclear power generation, chemical plants, air travel, drug safety, and residential development in hurricane or forest fire zones are all too risky to be left to private initiative and self-regulation. We need strong, well-resourced, well-staffed, and independent regulatory systems for these activities, and increasingly our scorecard on each of these dimensions is in the failing range.

This leads us to a fascinating question: is there a powerful constituency for health and safety within a democracy that could be a counterweight to corporate power and a bulwark for honest, scientifically guided regulatory regimes? Is a more level playing field between economic interests and the public's interests in effective safety regulation possible?

We may want to invoke the public at large, and it is true that public opinion is sometimes effective in demanding government intervention for safety. But the public is generally limited in several important ways. Only a small set of issues manage to become salient for the public. Further, issues only remain salient for a limited period of time. And the salience of an issue is often geographically and demographically bounded. There was intense opposition to the Shoreham nuclear plant siting decision on Long Island, but the public in Chicago and Dallas did not mobilize around the issue. Sometimes vocal public opinion prevails, but much more common is the scenario where public interest wanes and profit-motivated corporate interests persists. (Pepper Culpepper [2010] lays out the logic of salience and unequal power between a diffuse public and a concentrated corporate interest.)

Public interest organizations represent another pertinent voices for safety. Organizations like the Union of Concerned Scientists, Friends of the Earth, Bulletin of Atomic Scientists. Organizations have succeeded in creating a national base of support, they have drawn resources in support of their efforts, and they have a greater organizational capacity to persist over an extended period of time. (In another field of advocacy, organizations like Anti-Defamation League and the Southern Poverty Law Center have succeeded in maintaining organizational focus on the dangers of hate-based movements.) So public interest organizations sometimes have the capacity and staying power to advocate for stronger regulation.

Investigative journalism and a free press are also highly relevant in exposing regulatory failures and enhancing performance of safety organizations. *The New York Times* and *Washington Post* coverage of the FAA's role in certification of the 737 Max will almost certainly lead to improvements in this area of aircraft safety. The chronic failures of environmental, health, and safety regulation in authoritarian countries can be traced in large part to the fact that authoritarian states deny freedom of the press in their efforts to investigate and expose important failures by business or state enterprises.

Another important line of defense against undue influence by powerful outsiders is the set of regulations most governments and agencies have concerning conflict of interest and lobbying. These institutions certainly do not work perfectly; no one who pays attention would seriously think that agencies and governments are uninfluenced by gifts, contributions, promises of future benefits, and the blandishments of lobbyists. And these influences range from slight deviations to gross corruption. Moreover, influence does not need to be corrupt in order to be anti-democratic. If an energy company gets a privileged opportunity to make the case for "clean coal" behind closed doors, this may represent a legitimate set of partial arguments. The problem is that experts representing the public are not given the same opportunity.

A related mechanism is publicity, the expectation or requirement that decision-making agencies should make their deliberations and decision-making processes transparent and visible to the public. Let the public know who is influencing the debate, and perhaps this will deter decision-makers from favoring an important set of private interests. Then-Vice-President Cheney's refusal to make public the list of companies involved in consultations to the National Energy Policy Development Group is an instructive example; it is very natural to suspect that the recommendations put forward by the NEPDG reflected the specific business concerns of an unknown set of energy companies and lobbyists. So greater publicity of process can be a tool in enhancing the fit between policy and the public's interests.

THE NUCLEAR REGULATORY COMMISSION

The Nuclear Regulatory Commission (NRC) is an especially important example of the challenges facing government regulation, since the public depends on the NRC's ability to regulate and monitor the owners of especially hazardous and complex industrial processes. It is difficult to get an insider's perspective on the functioning of the NRC, but through many of its studies the Union of Concerned Scientists presents a fairly detailed and unbiased assessment of the NRC's ability to regulate nuclear power in the United States. And a detailed (and scathing) report by the General Accounting Office on the near-disaster at the Davis-Besse nuclear power plant is another expert assessment of NRC functioning (General Accounting Office 2004).

David Lochbaum et al. (2014) provide a detailed case history of the Fukushima nuclear disaster that also provides a degree of insight into the workings of the NRC as well as its Japanese counterpart. They provide a careful and scientific treatment of the unfolding of the Fukushima disaster hour by hour, and highlight the background errors that were made by regulators and owners in the design and operation of the Fukushima plant. The book makes numerous comparisons to the current workings of the NRC, which permit a degree of assessment of the US regulatory agency. In brief, Lochbaum and his co-authors appear to have a reasonably high opinion of the technical staff, scientists, and advisors who prepare recommendations for NRC consideration, but they express serious concerns about the willingness of the five commissioners to adopt costly recommendations that are strongly opposed by the nuclear industry. They note that the NRC has consistently declined to undertake more substantial reform of its approach to safety, as recommended by its own panel of experts. The key recommendation of the Near-Term Task Force (NTTF), established by the NRC to draw lessons for the United States from the experience of the Fukushima disaster, was that the regulatory framework should be anchored in a more strenuous standard of accident prevention, requiring plant owners to address "beyond-design-basis accidents". The Fukushima earthquake and tsunami events were "beyond-design-basis". Nonetheless, they occurred, and the NTTF recommended that safety planning should incorporate consideration of these unlikely but possible events.

Lochbaum and his co-authors express frustration that the nuclear safety agencies in both countries appear to have failed to have learned important lessons from the Fukushima disaster. They believe that the NRC is excessively vulnerable to influence by the nuclear power industry and to elected officials who favor economic growth over hypothetical safety concerns, with the result that it tends to err in favor of the economic interests of the industry. "Like many regulatory agencies, the NRC occupies uneasy ground between the need to guard public safety and the pressure from the industry it regulates to get off its back. When push comes to shove in that balancing act, the nuclear industry knows it can count on a sympathetic hearing in Congress; with millions of customers, the nation's nuclear utilities are an influential lobbying group" (Lochbaum et al. 2014: 36). As a result, "regulatory discipline" (essentially the pro-business ideology that holds that regulation should be kept to a minimum) prevailed, and the primary recommendation of the NTTF was tabled. The issue was of great importance, in that it involved setting the standard of risk and accident severity for which the owner needed to plan. By staying with the lower standard, the NRC left the door open to the most severe kinds of accidents. The authors argue that the NRC needs to significantly rethink its standards of safety and foreseeable risk. Their recommendation is to make use of an existing and rigorous plan for reactor safety incorporating the results of "severe accident mitigation alternatives" (SAMA) analysis already performed—but largely disregarded. However, they are not optimistic that the NRC will be willing to undertake these substantial changes that would significantly enhance safety and make a Fukushima-scale disaster less likely.

In addition to specific observations about the functioning of the NRC the authors identify chronic failures in the nuclear power system in Japan that should be of concern in the United States as well. Conflict of interest, falsification of records, and punishment of whistleblowers were part of the culture of nuclear power and nuclear regulation in Japan. And these problems can arise in the United States as well, as documented in the GAO report on the NRC's failures in the Davis-Besse near-accident (US GAO 2004).

There appear to be several structural factors that make nuclear regulation less effective than it needs to be. First is the fact of the political power and influence of the nuclear industry itself. Lochbaum and his collaborators demonstrate the power that TEPCO had in Japan in shaping the regulations under which it built the Fukushima complex, including the assumptions that were incorporated about earthquake risk and tsunami risk. Charles Perrow demonstrates a comparable ability by the nuclear industry in the United States to influence the rules and procedures that govern their use of nuclear power as well (Perrow 2011a). This influence permits the owners of nuclear power plants to influence the content of regulation as well as the systems of inspection and oversight that the agency adopts.

Third is the fact emphasized by Charles Perrow (2011a) that the NRC is primarily governed by Congress, and legislators are themselves vulnerable to the pressures and blandishments of the industry and demands for a low-regulation business environment. This makes it difficult for the NRC to carry out its role as independent guarantor of the health and safety of the public.

A fourth important factor is a pervasive complacency within the professional nuclear community about the inherent safety of nuclear power. This is an ideological or cultural factor, in that it describes a mental framework for thinking about the technology and the public. It is a very real factor in decision-making, both within the industry and in the regulatory world. Senior nuclear engineering experts at major research universities seem to share the view that the public "fear" of nuclear power is entirely misplaced, given the safety record of the industry. They believe the technical problems of nuclear power generation have been solved, and that a rational society would embrace nuclear power without anxiety. This professional complacency about nuclear safety makes safety regulation more difficult and, paradoxically, makes the safe use of nuclear power more unlikely. Only when the risks are confronted with complete transparency and honesty will it be possible to design regulatory systems that do an acceptable job of ensuring the safety and health of the public.

In short, Lochbaum and his colleagues at the Union of Concerned Scientists seem to provide evidence for the conclusion that the NRC is not in a position to perform at a high level of effectiveness its primary function: to establish a rational and scientifically well-grounded set of standards for safe reactor design and operation. Further, its ability to enforce through inspection seems impaired as well by the power and influence the nuclear industry can deploy through Congress to resist its regulatory efforts. Good expert knowledge is canvassed through the NRC's processes; but the policy recommendations that flow from this scientific analysis are all too often short-circuited by the ability of the industry to fend off new regulatory requirements.

Co-Regulation?

Is there a better approach to regulation of risky enterprises in a contemporary democracy? Can the problems of under-resourcing and industry capture be overcome? Balleisen and Eisner argue that the idea of *co-regulation* needs to be re-examined (Balleisen and Eisner 2009). They argue that this is not the same as "self-regulation"—turning over the task of regulating an industry to that industry itself. Rather, a system of co-regulation is one that establishes a strong relationship between public and private entities and maintains public accountability for the effectiveness of the regulatory regimes enacted by the private parties. "The problem often is not self-regulation per se, but the failure to integrate structures of private governance effectively within a larger institutional setting—to embed those structures within a broader framework of public oversight. In this chapter, we self-consciously use the term "co-regulation" to speak to the importance of integration and institutional design" (Balleisen and Eisner 2009: 129). Here is their more developed description of the arrangements they are considering:

> Private regulatory actors must possess genuine commitment to regulatory purposes, have a sufficient degree of institutional autonomy, and receive adequate resources to do their jobs properly. Equally important, they must be directed and constrained by a larger framework of "co-regulation." The state must furnish regulators with clear missions, and then maintain a close watch over those quasi-public or private regulators. To make such oversight efficacious, public regulators must receive accurate information about the activities of their private counterparts, and have sufficient expertise and capacity to assess the performance of nongovernmental regulators; and those nongovernmental regulators must face a credible threat that their public overseers will assume regulatory jurisdiction if they do not meet their obligations. It also helps if there is considerable transparency about the actions of quasi-public or private regulators that third parties can assist in the evaluation of regulatory performance. (129)

This system depends upon a strong and accountable relationship between the public authority and the private organization in whose hands the day-to-day regulatory work is vested. The public end of the regulatory system maintains oversight responsibility, and the nongovernmental regulator is subject to sanction if its processes are not sufficiently rigorous or effective. Here are the conditions that they believe determine the effectiveness of non-governmental regulatory regimes:

> The effectiveness of private regulation in a particular context—or, more precisely, the potential for credible co-regulation—depends on the following five factors: (1) the depth of concern for their reputation among regulated businesses; (2) the relevance of flexibility in regulatory detail; (3) the existence of sufficient bureaucratic capacity and autonomy on the part of nongovernmental regulators; (4) the degree of transparency in regulatory process; and (5) the seriousness of accountability. Before legislators

or regulatory agencies choose to delegate regulatory authority to industry organizations or corporations, they should assess the regulatory lay of the land with respect to each of these issues. (131)

They offer a few examples of promising "co-regulatory" experiments from the Clinton and Bush presidencies. One such experiment undertaken by the EPA was the National Environmental Performance Track (NEPT). "The EPA admits organizations to NEPT if they employ a high-quality environmental management system (EMS) assessed by third-party auditors using the EPA's assessment protocol, have a demonstrated commitment to continuous improvement, and have a strong record of compliance. The benefits of participation include: greater flexibility in compliance, streamlined permitting and reporting requirements, a lower inspection priority, and public recognition" (Balleisen and Eisner 2009: 140). They find the experience of NEPT to be moderately successful, with substantial reductions of pollution and greenhouse gases in the activities of member organizations.

Co-regulation sounds a lot like delegated regulation, and the same critical questions arise. How can we be confident that the regulations created and enforced by the nongovernmental regulator will *not* be subject to regulatory capture by the large companies subject to the regulations? When there is a legitimate difference of judgment about a safety regulation in the nuclear industry, what would give us confidence that the Institute of Nuclear Power Operators will give appropriate deference to the public's need for safety over the commercial interests of the operators? Balleisen and Eisner address these concerns by referring to the public institutions that must be created for a successful system of co-regulation; but this is precisely where the hardest issues arise, and their article does not give much of an idea of what those institutions might look like. However, Balleisen and Eisner make a good *prima facie* case that co-regulation is not the same as self-regulation or delegated regulation, in that it depends on a much more developed view of the organizational prerequisites on both the side of industry and government that would be needed in order for such a system to work. More empirical study would be needed, however, in order to assess whether this is an institutional arrangement that can succeed in overcoming the tendency towards regulatory capture by affected industries.

Andrew Hopkins describes a similar institutional arrangement concerning the relationship between government and industry in what he calls a "safety-case regime" theory of regulation (Hopkins 2000). This system appears to be similar to the institutions of co-regulation described by Balleisen and Eisner. Hopkins contrasts this approach with deregulation—the effort to allow the issue of safe operation to be governed by the market rather than by law. "Whereas the old-style legislation required employers to comply with precise, often quite technical rules, the new style imposes an overarching requirement on employers that they provide a safe and healthy workplace for their employees, as far as practicable" (Hopkins 2000: 92).

> The essence of the new approach is that the operator of a major hazard installation is required to make a case or demonstrate to the relevant authority that safety is being or will be effectively managed at the installation. Whereas under the self-regulatory approach, the facility operator is normally left to its own devices in deciding how to manage safety, under the safety case approach it must lay out its procedures for examination by the regulatory authority. (Hopkins 2000: 96)

A crucial part of management's responsibility under this system is to engage in formal "hazard and operability" (HAZOP) analysis for its industrial and environmental processes. "A HAZOP involves systematically imagining everything that might go wrong in a processing plant and developing procedures or engineering solutions to avoid these potential problems" (Hopkins 2000: 26). This kind of analysis is especially critical in high-risk industries including chemical plants, petrochemical refineries, and nuclear reactors. The preparation of a safety case includes a comprehensive HAZOP analysis, along with procedures for preventing or responding to the occurrence of possible hazards. Once the industry's safety case has been approved and adopted by the government agency, the industry is legally liable for performing in accordance with its specifications. Hopkins reports that the safety case approach to regulation is being adopted by the EU, Australia, and the UK with respect to a number of high-risk industries. He notes that this approach does not necessarily reduce the need for government inspections; but the goal of regulatory inspection will be different. Inspectors will seek to satisfy themselves that the industry has done a responsible job of identifying hazards and planning accordingly, rather than looking for violations of specific rules. (Hopkins provides more detail about the workings of a safety case regime in his treatment of the Deepwater Horizon disaster [2012: chapter 10].)

This discussion is highly relevant to new debates about how a regulatory system can be more effective.

Closing

What insights emerge from the discussions of this chapter for the ontology of policy implementation and executive decisions? Like all organizational processes, policy formulation and implementation proceeds through individual actors in particular circumstances guided by particular interests and preferences; implementation is likely to be imperfect in the best of circumstances and entirely ineffectual in other circumstances; implementation is affected by the strategic non-governmental actors and organizations it is designed to influence, leading to further distortion and incompleteness. We can also, more positively, identify specific mechanisms that governments and executives can introduce to increase the effectiveness of implementation of their policies. These include internal audit and discipline functions, communications strategies designed at enhancing conformance by intermediate actors, encouragement and protection of whistle-blowers, periodic purges of non-conformant sub-officials and powerful non-governmental actors, and dozens of other strategies and mechanisms of conformance.

Most fundamentally we can say that any model of government that postulates frictionless application and implementation of policy is flawed at its core. Such a model overlooks an ontological fundamental about government and other organizations, large and small: that organizational action is never automatic, algorithmic, or exact; that it is always conveyed by intermediate actors who have their own understandings and preferences about policy; and that it works in an environment where powerful non-governmental actors are almost always in positions to blunt the effectiveness of "the will of government".

References

Balleisen, Edward J., and Marc Eisner. "The Promise and Pitfalls of Co-Regulation: How Governments Can Draw on Private Governance for Public Purpose." In *New Perspectives on Regulation*, edited by David A. Moss and John A. Cisternino, 127–50. Cambridge, MA: The Tobin Project, 2009.

Culpepper, Pepper. *Quiet Politics and Business Power: Corporate Control in Europe and Japan*. Cambridge; New York: Cambridge University Press, 2010.

Engels, Friedrich. *The Condition of the Working Class in England*. Edited and translated by W.O. Henderson and W.H. Chaloner. Oxford: B. Blackwell, 1958 [1845].

Fligstein, Neil, and Doug McAdam. *A Theory of Fields*. New York: Oxford University Press, 2012.

General Accounting Office. *Nuclear Regulation: NRC Needs to More Aggressively and Comprehensively Resolve Issues Related to the Davis-Besse Nuclear Power Plant's Shutdown*. GAO-04-415. GAO, 2004.

Hopkins, Andrew. *Lessons from Longford: The ESSO Gas Plant Explosion*. Macquarie, Australia: CCH Australia, 2000.

Hopkins, Andrew. *Failure to Learn: The BP Texas City Refinery Disaster*. Macquarie, Australia: CCH Australia, 2008.

Hopkins, Andrew. *Disastrous Decisions: The Human and Organisational Causes of the Gulf of Mexico Blowout*. Macquarie, Australia: CCH Australia, 2012.

Lochbaum, David, Edwin Lyman, Susan D. Stranahan, and Union of Concerned Scientists. *Fukushima: The Story of a Nuclear Disaster*. New York: The New Press, 2014.

Perrow, Charles. Fukushima and the Inevitability of Accidents, Bulletin of the Atomic Scientists. December 1, 2011a. https://thebulletin.org/2011/12/fukushima-and-the-inevitability-of-accidents/.

Perrow, Charles. *The Next Catastrophe: Reducing Our Vulnerabilities to Natural, Industrial, and Terrorist Disasters*. Princeton: Princeton University Press, 2011b.

Raso, Connor. "Boeing Crisis Illustrates Risks of Delegated Regulatory Authority." *Brookings*, Regulatory Process and Perspective, 2019.

Stiglitz, Joseph E. "Regulation and Failure." In *New Perspectives on Regulation*, edited by David A. Moss and John A. Cisternino, 11–24. Cambridge, MA: The Tobin Project, 2009.

US Government Accountability Office. *Nuclear Regulation: NRC Needs to More Aggressively and Comprehensively Resolve Issues Related to the Davis-Besse Nuclear Power Plant's Shutdown*. Washington, DC: U.S. Government, 2004. www.gao.gov/cgi-bin/getrpt?GAO-04-415.

CHAPTER 10

Concluding Observations

Abstract This chapter reviews several substantive ideas. First, the ontology of government proposed here is actor-centered. The properties and activities of government are generated by the socially-constituted actors who make up the offices and agencies of government. Second, we can understand much of the workings of governments through the findings of institutional sociology and organizational studies. Government is an assemblage of organizations, with social networks, authority relations, and modes of influence and culture that influence and shape the behavior of the actors within the organizations of government. Third, government is inherently complex. It is a network of organizations encompassing many mechanisms of information gathering and analysis, priority setting, policy writing, regulation, and enforcement. Throughout we have seen that these particulars of the composition of government give rise to the perennial possibility of dysfunction. All of these dysfunctions can be addressed, and indeed, many improvements are underway at present at multiple levels of government and civil society. However, it is clear that effective government is a dynamic and never-ending project.

Keywords Social ontology · Government · Democracy · Organizational studies · Actor-centered sociology · New institutionalism

This book has introduced several substantive ideas that are useful to describe and explain the workings of government: power, authority, role, agency, social network, assemblage, strategic action field, interest, culture, norms, goals, and institutions. Government consists of a set of elected officials, directors, professional staff, and other employees, located within agencies and departments, with overall legitimacy deriving from the democratic institutions through which it is formed and evaluated.

These ideas contribute to an overarching conception of government within a democracy. First, our ontology is actor-centered. The properties and activities of government are generated by the socially-constituted actors who make up the offices and agencies of government. The actors within government possess knowledge and their own sets of goals and priorities, even as they are influenced by the goals and directions of their agency. Actors (employees) have specified roles within their agency, along with work expectations aligned with the specified role. Actors are supervised by individuals who themselves stand in a system of authority, accountability, culture, and reward. Authority relations do not fully determine the actions of individuals throughout the system.

Second, we can understand much of the workings of governments through the findings of institutional sociology and organizational studies. Government is an assemblage of organizations, with social networks, authority relations, and modes of influence and culture that influence and shape the behavior of the actors within the organizations of government. Governments consist of actors enmeshed within authority systems, networks of collaboration, communication, and coordination, and large ensembles of cultural values and norms. There is a "logic of institutions" and a set of patterns of organizational behavior that we can discover in the workings of government.

Third, government is inherently complex. It is a network of organizations encompassing many mechanisms of information gathering and analysis, priority setting, policy writing, regulation, and enforcement. Mechanisms of authority and coordination extend across this network, linking many thousands of individuals in the work of government. Electoral politics represents an important mechanism as well, in that candidates compete over issues that the electorate cares about, and this competition has deep effects on the nature of the policies and behaviors that result from governmental processes. There are relations of power and authority that extend vertically and horizontally within government, with meaningful levels of independence in various agencies.

10 CONCLUDING OBSERVATIONS   163

The fundamental characteristics of government action can be addressed by thinking about the individuals who make up various units and agencies of government; the values, motivations, and beliefs that they bring to their work; the institutional arrangements within which they work; the arrangements that address principal-agent problems and establish a degree of compliance within the organization; the ways in which different sets of goals and interests are impressed upon the agency by powerful insiders and outsiders; and the ways in which the agency exercises power and influence to enact the policies that it has created. This is the thrust of the actor-centered approach to social ontology that has guided much of the argument of this book: actors within a given set of institutional circumstances carry out their own plans of work in the creation and execution of public policy.

Throughout we have seen that these particulars of the circumstances of organization and agency in government give rise to the perennial possibility of dysfunction. The sources of dysfunction are now familiar: conflicting priorities among influential leaders; faulty communication across agencies; extensive and effective efforts by powerful outsiders to influence government action; imperfect ability by "principals" to control the actions of their "agents" in the pursuit of government purposes; potential conflicts of interest at every level of government action; and imperfect capacity within government to formulate and adopt scientific and evidence-based conclusions about complex policy issues. All these organizational and human failings show up in the activities of government. A central tenet of this book is that dysfunction is inevitable in large, complex forms of social coordination and administration, much as Charles Perrow finds that accidents are "normal" in complex industrial systems. These conclusions are true in the context of large private organizations such as business corporations and non-profit organizations. And because of the size, complexity, and multi-valenced goals of actors within government, the same conclusions apply to the activities of government as well. Organizations, authority structures, and networks of collaboration and coordination are all imperfect in their ability to control the actions of myriad officials, policy makers, scientists, and inspectors, and the results of government activity often fall far short of what might be described as "ideal implementation of the public good". This is not to say that governments are incapable of achieving good results and are unreliable stewards of the public good. It is only to recognize the organizational failures that are possible, even likely, in any large system of social coordination.

Many of these dysfunctions can be addressed in familiar ways. It is possible to redesign important government organizations in such a way as to make them more effective systems for achieving their goals. It is possible to improve the "culture" of the government workplace so that conflicts of interest and mismatches of priorities are minimized. It is possible to enhance the ability of the public to observe the manipulations of government by powerful private interests so that democratic pressure can be brought to bear in support of the public good. It is possible to encourage whistle-blowers and investigative journalists alike to shed light on the hidden processes of government decision-making in ways that enhance transparency and encourages actions aligned with the public good.

All of these improvements are possible, and indeed, many are underway at present at multiple levels of government and civil society. Effective government is a dynamic and never-ending project. In the end, however, it is crucial for citizens and officials alike to have a good understanding of the mechanisms and influences that are at work within government action and their failure modalities, and to pay particular attention to effective performance in the areas that matter most to securing the public good.

REFERENCES

Anheier, Helmut K., ed. *When Things Go Wrong: Organizational Failures and Breakdowns*. Thousand Oaks, CA: Sage, 1999.
Archer, Margaret Scotford. *Realist Social Theory: The Morphogenetic Approach*. Cambridge; New York: Cambridge University Press, 1995.
Archer, Margaret Scotford, ed. *Culture and Agency: The Place of Culture in Social Theory*. Rev. Cambridge, UK; New York, NY, USA: Cambridge University Press, 1996.
Archer, Margaret Scotford, ed. *Critical Realism: Essential Readings*. Critical Realism–Interventions. London; New York: Routledge, 1998.
Archer, Margaret S., Claire Decoteau, Philip Gorski, Daniel Little, Doug Porpora, Timothy Rutzou, Christian Smith, George Steinmetz, and Frederic Vandenberghe. "What Is Critical Realism?" *Perspectives* 38, no. 2 (2016): 4–9.
Bachrach, Peter, and Morton S. Baratz. "Two Faces of Power." *American Political Science Review* 56, no. 4 (1962): 947–52.
Balleisen, Edward J., and Marc Eisner. "The Promise and Pitfalls of Co-Regulation: How Governments Can Draw on Private Governance for Public Purpose." In *New Perspectives on Regulation*, edited by David A. Moss and John A. Cisternino, 127–50. Cambridge, MA: The Tobin Project, 2009.
Bates, Robert H. *Markets and States in Tropical Africa: The Political Basis of Agricultural Policies*. Berkeley: University of California Press, 1981.
Bauman, Zygmunt. *Liquid Modernity*. 2nd ed. Cambridge, UK; Malden, MA: Polity Press; Blackwell, 2012.

Beekun, Rafik, and William H. Glick. "Organization Structure from a Loose Coupling Perspective: A Multidimensional Approach." *Decision Sciences* 32, no. 2 (2001): 227–50.

Berger, Michele, and Kathleen Guidroz, eds. *The Intersectional Approach Transforming the Academy Through Race, Class, and Gender*. Chapel Hill: University of North Carolina Press, 2009.

Bhaskar, Roy. *A Realist Theory of Science*. Leeds: Leeds Books, 1975.

Bhaskar, Roy. *The Possibility of Naturalism: A Philosophical Critique of the Human Sciences*. 2nd ed. London: Harvester Wheatsheaf, 1989.

Bhaskar, Roy. *Dialectic: The Pulse of Freedom*. London; New York: Verso, 1993.

Bovens, Mark, and Paul 't Hart. *Understanding Policy Fiascoes*. London: Routledge, 2017.

Boyd, Richard. "Materialism Without Reductionism: What Physicalism Does Not Entail." In *Readings in the Philosophy of Psychology Vol. 1*, edited by Ned Block. Cambridge, MA: Harvard University Press, 1980.

Boyd, Richard. "Realism, Approximate Truth, and Philosophical Method." In *Scientific Theories*, edited by C. Wade Savage. Minneapolis: University of Minnesota Press, 1990.

Brinton, Mary C., and Victor Nee, eds. *New Institutionalism in Sociology*. New York: Russell Sage Foundation, 1998.

Bunge, Mario. "Mechanism and Explanation." *Philosophy of the Social Sciences* 27, no. 4 (1997): 410–65.

Burguière, André. *The Annales School: An Intellectual History*. Ithaca, NY: Cornell University Press, 2009.

Cameron, Kim S. *Competing Values Leadership: Creating Value in Organizations*. New Horizons in Management. Cheltenham, UK; Northampton, MA: Edward Elgar, 2006.

Cameron, Kim S. *Organizational Effectiveness*. Cheltenham; Northhampton, MA: Edward Elgar, 2010.

Case, Anne, and Angus Deaton. *Mortality and Morbidity in the 21st Century*. Brookings Papers on Economic Activity, Spring, 2017.

Clarke, Lee, and Charles Perrow. "Prosaic Organizational Failure." *American Behavioral Scientist* 39, no. 8 (1996): 1040–56.

Coase, R. H. *The Firm, the Market, and the Law*. Chicago: University of Chicago Press, 1988.

Cohen, Eliot, and John Gooch. *Military Misfortunes: The Anatomy of Failure in War*. New York: Vintage, 1990.

Coleman, James S. *Foundations of Social Theory*. Cambridge: Harvard University Press, 1990.

Cronon, William. *Nature's Metropolis: Chicago and the Great West*. New York: W. W. Norton, 1991.

Crozier, Michel, and Erhard Friedberg. *Actors and Systems: The Politics of Collective Action*. Chicago: University of Chicago Press, 1980.

Culpepper, Pepper. *Quiet Politics and Business Power: Corporate Control in Europe and Japan*. Cambridge; New York: Cambridge University Press, 2010.

Dahl, Robert A. "The Concept of Power." *Behavioral Science* 2, no. 3 (1957): 201–15.

De Vries, Michiel S. *The Importance of Neglect in Policy-Making*. London; New York: Palgrave Macmillan, 2010.

DeLanda, Manuel. *A New Philosophy of Society: Assemblage Theory and Social Complexity*. London; New York: Continuum International Publishing Group, 2006.

Deleuze, Gilles, and Félix Guattari. *A Thousand Plateaus: Capitalism and Schizophrenia*. Minneapolis: University of Minnesota Press, 1987.

Diani, Mario, and Doug McAdam, eds. *Social Movements and Networks: Relational Approaches to Collective Action*. Comparative Politics. Oxford; New York: Oxford University Press, 2003.

Dobbin, Frank. *Forging Industrial Policy: The United States, Britain, and France in the Railway Age*. Cambridge, UK; New York: Cambridge University Press, 1994.

Domhoff, G. William. *The Higher Circles; the Governing Class in America*. 1st ed. New York: Random House, 1970.

Dye, Thomas R. *Who's Running America? The Obama Reign*. 18th ed. London: Routledge, 2014.

Dye, Thomas R., Harmon Zeigler, and Louis Schubert. *The Irony of Democracy: An Uncommon Introduction to American Politics*. 15th ed. Boston: Cengage Learning, 2011.

Ehrenreich, Barbara. *Nickel and Dimed: On (Not) Getting by in America*. 1st ed. New York: Metropolitan Books, 2001.

Elder-Vass, David. *The Causal Power of Social Structures: Emergence, Structure and Agency*. Cambridge: Cambridge University Press, 2010.

Elster, Jon. *Nuts and Bolts for the Social Sciences*. Cambridge: Cambridge University Press, 1989.

Engels, Friedrich. *The Condition of the Working Class in England*. Edited and translated by W.O. Henderson and W.H. Chaloner. Oxford: B. Blackwell, 1958 [1845].

Epstein, Brian. "Ontological Individualism Reconsidered." *Synthese* 166 (2009): 187–213.

Epstein, Joshua. *Generative Social Science: Studies in Agent-Based Computational Modeling*. Princeton, NJ: Princeton University Press, 2006.

Esping-Andersen, Gosta. *Politics Against Markets: The Social Democratic Road to Power*. Princeton: Princeton University Press, 1985.

Fligstein, Neil, and Doug McAdam. "Toward a General Theory of Strategic Action Fields." *Sociological Theory* 29, no. 1 (2011): 1–26.
Fligstein, Neil, and Doug McAdam. *A Theory of Fields*. New York: Oxford University Press, 2012.
Fodor, Jerry. "Special Sciences and the Disunity of Science as a Working Hypothesis." *Synthese* 28, no. 2 (1974): 97–115.
Fung, Archon, and Erik Olin Wright. *Deepening Democracy: Institutional Innovations in Empowered Participatory Governance*. The Real Utopias Project 4. London: Verso, 2003.
Geertz, Clifford. *Islam Observed; Religious Development in Morocco and Indonesia*. New Haven: Yale University Press, 1968.
Geertz, Clifford. *The Interpretation of Cultures; Selected Essays*. New York: Basic Books, 1971.
General Accounting Office. *Nuclear Regulation: NRC Needs to More Aggressively and Comprehensively Resolve Issues Related to the Davis-Besse Nuclear Power Plant's Shutdown*. GAO-04-415. GAO, 2004.
Gest, Justin. *The New Minority: White Working Class Politics in an Age of Immigration and Inequality*. Oxford; New York: Oxford University Press, 2016.
Gibbard, Allan. *Wise Choices, Apt Feelings: A Theory of Normative Judgment*. Cambridge: Harvard University Press, 1990.
Giddens, Anthony. *Central Problems in Social Theory: Action, Structure and Contradiction in Social Analysis*. Berkeley: University of California Press, 1979.
Granovetter, Mark. "Economic Action and Social Structure: The Problem of Embeddedness." *American Journal of Sociology* 91, no. 3 (1985): 481–510.
Green, Donald P., and Ian Shapiro. *Pathologies of Rational Choice Theory: A Critique of Applications in Political Science*. New Haven: Yale University Press, 1994.
Gutmann, Amy, and Dennis Thompson. *Why Deliberative Democracy?* Princeton, NJ: Princeton University Press, 2004.
Guzzetti, Jeffrey B. *FAA Needs to Strengthen Its Risk Assessment and Oversight Approach for Organization Designation Authorization and Risk-Based Resource Targeting Programs*. AV-2011-136. Office of Inspector General, Department of Transportation, 2011.
Hagedorn, Sara. "Taking the Lead: Congressional Staffers and Their Role in the Policy Process." PhD dissertation, University of Colorado, 2015.
Harré, Rom. *Principles of Scientific Thinking*. Chicago: University of Chicago, 1970.
Hedström, Peter. *Dissecting the Social: On the Principles of Analytical Sociology*. Cambridge, UK; New York: Cambridge University Press, 2005.

Hedström, Peter, and Richard Swedberg, eds. *Social Mechanisms: An Analytical Approach to Social Theory*. Studies in Rationality and Social Change. Cambridge, UK; New York: Cambridge University Press, 1998.

Hellriegel, Don, and John W. Slocum. *Organizational Behavior*. 12th ed. Mason, OH: South-Western Cengage Learning, 2009.

Hess, David J. "Catalyzing Corporate Commitment to Combating Corruption." *Journal of Business Ethics* 88 (2009): 781–90.

Hess, David. "Combating Corruption in International Business: The Big Questions." *Ohio Northern Law Review* 41, no. 3 (2015): 679–96.

Hess, David. "Ethical Infrastructures and Evidence-Based Corporate Compliance and Ethics Programs: Policy Implications from the Empirical Evidence." *New York University Journal of Law & Business* 12, no. 2 (2016): 317–68.

Hill, Lance E. *The Deacons for Defense: Armed Resistance and the Civil Rights Movement*. Chapel Hill: University of North Carolina Press, 2004.

Hofstede, Geert. *Culture's Consequences: Comparing Values, Behaviors, Institutions, and Organizations across Nations*. 2nd ed. Sage, 2003.

Hopkins, Andrew. *Lessons from Longford: The ESSO Gas Plant Explosion*. Macquarie, Australia: CCH Australia, 2000.

Hopkins, Andrew. *Failure to Learn: The BP Texas City Refinery Disaster*. Macquarie, Australia: CCH Australia, 2008.

Hopkins, Andrew. *Disastrous Decisions: The Human and Organisational Causes of the Gulf of Mexico Blowout*. Macquarie, Australia: CCH Australia, 2012.

Hughes, Thomas Parke. *Rescuing Prometheus*. 1st ed. New York: Pantheon Books, 1998.

Kadushin, Charles. *Understanding Social Networks: Theories, Concepts, and Findings*. Oxford; New York: Oxford University Press, 2012.

Kahneman, Daniel, Paul Slovic, and Amos Tversky. *Judgment under Uncertainty: Heuristics and Biases*. Cambridge: Cambridge University Press, 1982.

Kaidesoja, Tuukka. *Naturalizing Critical Realist Social Ontology*. London: Routledge, 2013.

Kim, Jaegwon. *Supervenience and Mind: Selected Philosophical Essays*. Cambridge: Cambridge University Press, 1993.

Klitgaard, Robert E. *Controlling Corruption*. Berkeley: University of California Press, 1988.

Klitgaard, Robert E. *Addressing Corruption Together*. Paris: OECD Development Centre, 2015.

Knight, Jack. *Institutions and Social Conflict*. The Political Economy of Institutions and Decisions. Cambridge, UK; New York, NY: Cambridge University Press, 1992.

Knight, Jack, and Jim Johnson. *The Priority of Democracy: Political Consequences of Pragmatism*. Princeton, NJ: Princeton University Press, 2012.

Leplin, Jarrett, ed. *Scientific Realism*. Berkeley: University of California Press, 1984.
Little, Daniel. *Varieties of Social Explanation: An Introduction to the Philosophy of Social Science*. Boulder, CO: Westview Press, 1991.
Little, Daniel. *Microfoundations, Method and Causation: On the Philosophy of the Social Sciences*. New Brunswick, NJ: Transaction Publishers, 1998.
Little, Daniel. "Levels of the Social." In *Handbook for Philosophy of Anthropology and Sociology*, edited by Stephen Turner and Mark Risjord, 15, 343–71. Handbook of the Philosophy of Science. Amsterdam; New York: Elsevier Publishing, 2006.
Little, Daniel. "Causal Mechanisms in the Social Realm." In *Causality in the Sciences*, edited by Phyllis Illari, Federica Russo, and Jon Williamson. Oxford: Oxford University Press, 2011.
Little, Daniel. "Supervenience and the Social World." *Metodo* 3, no. 2 (2015): 125–45.
Little, Daniel. *New Directions in the Philosophy of Social Science*. London: Rowman & Littlefield Publishers, 2016.
Little, Daniel. "Microfoundations." In *The Routledge Companion to Philosophy of Social Science*, edited by Lee McIntyre and Alex Rosenberg. London; New York: Routledge, 2017.
Lochbaum, David, Edwin Lyman, Susan D. Stranahan, and Union of Concerned Scientists. *Fukushima: The Story of a Nuclear Disaster*. New York: The New Press, 2014.
Luhmann, Niklas, Dirk Baecker, and Peter Gilgen. *Introduction to Systems Theory*. Cambridge, UK; Malden, MA: Polity, 2013.
Lukes, Steven. *Power: A Radical View*. 2nd ed. London; New York: Macmillan, 2005 [1974].
Mahoney, James. "Beyond Correlational Analysis: Recent Innovations in Theory and Method." *Sociological Forum* 16, no. 3 (2001): 575–93.
Mahoney, James, and Kathleen Ann Thelen. *Explaining Institutional Change: Ambiguity, Agency, and Power*. Cambridge; New York: Cambridge University Press, 2010.
Manicas, Peter T. *A Realist Philosophy of Social Science: Explanation and Understanding*. Cambridge, UK; New York: Cambridge University Press, 2006.
Mann, Michael. *The Sources of Social Power. A History of Power from the Beginning to A.D. 1760*. Vol. 1. Cambridge: Cambridge University Press, 1986.
Mann, Michael. *Fascists*. New York: Cambridge University Press, 2004.
March, James G., and Herbert A. Simon. *Organizations*. New York: Wiley, 1958.

March, James G., and Johan P. Olsen. "The New Institutionalism: Organizational Factors in Political Life." *American Political Science Review* 78, no. 3 (1984): 734–49.
Martin, Joanne. *Organizational Culture: Mapping the Terrain (Foundations for Organizational Science)*. Joanne Martin: Sage, 2001.
Marx, Karl. "The Eighteenth Brumaire of Louis Bonaparte." In *Surveys from Exile*, edited by David Fernbach. New York: Vintage, 1974.
Marx, Karl, and Frederick Engels. "The Communist Manifesto." In *The Revolutions of 1848: Political Writings, Vol. I.*, edited by David Fernbach. New York: Vintage, 1974.
McAdam, Doug. *Political Process and the Development of Black Insurgency, 1930–1970*. 2nd ed. Chicago: University of Chicago Press, 1999.
McAdam, Doug, and Karina Kloos. *Deeply Divided: Racial Politics and Social Movements in Postwar America*. Oxford; New York: Oxford University Press, 2014.
McAdam, Doug, Sidney G. Tarrow, and Charles Tilly. *Dynamics of Contention*. New York: Cambridge University Press, 2001.
McGinnis, Michael D., and Elinor Ostrom. "Social-Ecological System Framework: Initial Changes and Continuing Challenges." *Ecology and Society* 19, no. 2 (2014): art. 30.
Merton, Robert K. "On Sociological Theories of the Middle Range." In *Social Theory and Social Structure*, edited by Robert K. Merton. New York: Free Press, 1963.
Miliband, Ralph. "Marx and the State." *The Socialist Register*, 1965.
Miliband, Ralph. *The State in Capitalist Society*. New York: Basic, 1969.
Miller, John H., and Scott E. Page. *Complex Adaptive Systems: An Introduction to Computational Models of Social Life*. Princeton: Princeton University Press, 2007.
Mills, C. Wright. *The Power Elite*. New York: Oxford University Press, 1956.
Morçöl, Göktuğ. *A Complexity Theory for Public Policy*. London: Routledge, 2012.
Moss, David A., and John A. Cisternino, eds. *New Perspectives on Regulation*. Cambridge, MA: The Tobin Project, 2009.
Mounk, Yascha. *The People vs. Democracy: Why Our Freedom Is in Danger and How to Save It*. Cambridge: Harvard University Press, 2018.
Mudde, Cas. *The Far Right Today*. Cambridge, UK; Malden, MA: Polity, 2019.
Mudde, Cas, and Cristobal Rovira Kaltwasser. *Populism: A Very Short Introduction*. 2nd ed. Oxford; New York: Oxford University Press, 2017.
National Academies of Sciences, Engineering, and Medicine. *Sexual Harassment of Women: Climate, Culture, and Consequences in Academic Sciences, Engineering, and Medicine*. Washington, DC: The National Academies Press, 2018. https://doi.org/10.17226/24994.

Niiniluoto, Ilkka. *Critical Scientific Realism*. Oxford; New York: Oxford University Press, 1999.

Ocasio, William, Patricia H. Thornton, and Michael Lounsbury. "Advances to the Institutional Logics Perspective." In *Sage Handbook of Organizational Institutionalism*. 2nd ed. London; Thousand Oaks, CA: Sage, 2017.

Oreskes, Naomi, and Erik M. Conway. *Merchants of Doubt: How a Handful of Scientists Obscured the Truth on Issues from Tobacco Smoking to Global Warming*. New York: Bloomsbury Press, 2010.

Oreskes, Naomi, Dale Jamieson, Keynyn Brysse, Jessica O'Reilly, Matthew Shindell, and Milena Wazeck. *Discerning Experts: The Practices of Scientific Assessment for Environmental Policy*. Chicago; London: University of Chicago Press, 2019.

Ornstein, Norm. "The Real Story of Obamacare's Birth." *The Atlantic*, July 6, 2015.

Orton, J. Douglas, and Karl E. Weick. "Loosely Coupled Systems: A Reconceptualization." *Academy of Management Review* 15, no. 2 (1990): 203–23.

Ostrom, Elinor. *Governing the Commons: The Evolution of Institutions for Collective Action*. Cambridge, UK; New York: Cambridge University Press, 1990.

Page, Scott E. *The Difference: How the Power of Diversity Creates Better Groups, Firms, Schools, and Societies*. Princeton: Princeton University Press, 2007.

Perrow, Charles. *Normal Accidents: Living with High-Risk Technologies—With a New Afterword and a Postscript on the Y2K Problem*. Princeton, NJ: Princeton University Press, 1999 [1984].

Perrow, Charles. *Organizing America: Wealth, Power, and the Origins of Corporate Capitalism*. Princeton, NJ: Princeton University Press, 2002.

Perrow, Charles. Fukushima and the Inevitability of Accidents, Bulletin of the Atomic Scientists. December 1, 2011a. https://thebulletin.org/2011/12/fukushima-and-the-inevitability-of-accidents/.

Perrow, Charles. *The Next Catastrophe: Reducing Our Vulnerabilities to Natural, Industrial, and Terrorist Disasters*. Princeton: Princeton University Press, 2011b.

Perrow, Charles. *Complex Organizations: A Critical Essay*. 3rd ed. Brattleboro, VT: Echo Point Books and Media, 2014 [1972].

Pierson, Paul. *Politics in Time: History, Institutions, and Social Analysis*. Princeton: Princeton University Press, 2004.

Porpora, Doug. *Reconstructing Sociology: The Critical Realist Approach*. Cambridge; New York, NY: Cambridge University Press, 2015.

Poulantzas, Nicos. *Political Power and Social Class*. London: New Left Books, 1973.

Powell, Walter, and Paul J. DiMaggio. *The New Institutionalism in Organizational Analysis*. Chicago: University of Chicago Press, 1991.

Putnam, Robert D. *Bowling Alone: The Collapse and Revival of American Community.* New York: Simon & Schuster, 2000.
Raadschelders, Jos C. N. *Public Administration: The Interdisciplinary Study of Government.* Paperback Edition. Oxford; New York: Oxford University Press, 2013.
Raadschelders, Jos C. N. *What Is Government? Human Instinct, Tribal Community, Global Society.* Ann Arbor: University of Michigan Press, 2020.
Raadschelders, Jos C. N., and Travis A. Whetsell. "Conceptualizing the Landscape of Decision Making for Complex Problem Solving." *International Journal of Public Administration* 41, no. 14 (2018): 1132–44.
Raso, Connor. "Boeing Crisis Illustrates Risks of Delegated Regulatory Authority." *Brookings*, Regulatory Process and Perspective, 2019.
Rodwin, Marc. *Conflicts of Interest and the Future of Medicine in the United States, France, and Japan.* Oxford; New York: Oxford University Press, 2011.
Sabel, Charles F., and Jonathan Zeitlin. *Worlds of Possibility: Flexibility and Mass Production in Western Industrialization.* Cambridge, UK; New York: Maison des sciences de l'homme: Cambridge University Press, 1997.
Sagan, Scott Douglas. *The Limits of Safety: Organizations, Accidents, and Nuclear Weapons.* Princeton, NJ: Princeton University Press, 1993.
Schein, Edgar, and Peter Schein. *Organizational Culture and Leadership.* 5th ed. New York: Jossey-Bass, 2016 [1990].
Scott, W. Richard. *Organizations: Rational, Natural, and Open Systems.* Englewood Cliffs, NJ: Prentice-Hall, 1981.
Scott, W. Richard. *Institutions and Organizations.* Thousand Oaks, CA: Sage, 1995.
Scott, W. Richard, and Gerald F. Davis. *Organizations and Organizing: Rational, Natural, and Open System Perspectives.* 1st ed. Upper Saddle River, NJ: Pearson Prentice Hall, 2007.
Sen, Amartya. "Rational Fools: A Critique of the Behavioral Foundations of Economic Theory." *Philosophy & Public Affairs* 6, no. 4 (1977): 317–44.
Simon, Herbert. "The Architecture of Complexity." *Proceedings of the American Philosophical Society* 106, no. 6 (1962): 467–82.
Simon, Herbert A. *Administrative Behavior: A Study of Decision-Making Processes in Administrative Organizations.* 4th ed. New York: Free Press, 1997 [1947].
Stever, Donald W. Jr. *Seabrook and the Nuclear Regulatory Commission: The Licensing of a Nuclear Power Plant.* University Press of New England, 1980.
Stiglitz, Joseph E. "Principal and Agent." In *The New Palgrave: A Dictionary of Economics*, edited by John Eatwell, Murray Milgate, and Peter Newman. 3rd ed., 966–71. London: Palgrave Macmillan, 1987.
Stiglitz, Joseph E. "Principal and Agent." In *Allocation, Information and Markets*, edited by John Eatwell, Murray Milgate, and Peter Newman, 241–53. The New Palgrave. London: Palgrave Macmillan, 1989.

Stiglitz, Joseph E. "Regulation and Failure." In *New Perspectives on Regulation*, edited by David A. Moss and John A. Cisternino, 11–24. Cambridge, MA: The Tobin Project, 2009.

Thelen, Kathleen Ann. *How Institutions Evolve: The Political Economy of Skills in Germany, Britain, the United States, and Japan*. Cambridge Studies in Comparative Politics. Cambridge; New York: Cambridge University Press, 2004.

Thelen, Kathleen, and James Conran. "Institutional Change." In *The Oxford Handbook of Historical Institutionalism*, edited by Orfeo Fioretos, Tulia G. Falleti, and Adam Sheingate. Oxford; New York: Oxford University Press, 2016.

Thompson, Dennis F. "Understanding Financial Conflicts of Interest." *New England Journal of Medicine* 329, no. 8 (1993): 573–76.

Thornton, Patricia H., and William Ocasio. "Institutional Logics." In *The SAGE Handbook of Organizational Institutionalism*, edited by Royston Greenwood, Christine Oliver, Roy Suddaby, and Kerstin Sahlin-Andersson, 1st ed. Thousand Oaks, CA: Sage, 2008.

Thornton, Patricia H., William Ocasio, and Michael Lounsbury. *The Institutional Logics Perspective: A New Approach to Culture, Structure, and Process*. Oxford: Oxford University Press, 2012.

Tierney, Kathleen J. *The Social Roots of Risk Producing Disasters, Promoting Resilience*. Stanford, CA: Stanford Business Books, an Imprint of Stanford University Press, 2014.

Tilly, Charles. "To Explain Political Processes." *American Journal of Sociology* 100 (1995): 1594–1610.

US EPA. *Respiratory Health Effects of Passive Smoking: Lung Cancer and Other Disorders*. EPA/600/6-90/006F. Washington, DC: US EPA Federal Registry, 1992.

US Government Accountability Office. *Nuclear Regulation: NRC Needs to More Aggressively and Comprehensively Resolve Issues Related to the Davis-Besse Nuclear Power Plant's Shutdown*. Washington, DC: U.S. Government, 2004. www.gao.gov/cgi-bin/getrpt?GAO-04-415.

Vaughan, Diane. *The Challenger Launch Decision: Risky Technology, Culture, and Deviance at NASA*. Chicago: University of Chicago Press, 1996.

Warshaw, Shirley Anne. *The Domestic Presidency: Policy Making in the White House*. Needham Heights, MA: Allyn & Bacon, 1997.

Weick, Karl E. "Educational Organizations as Loosely Coupled Systems." *Administrative Science Quarterly* 21, no. 1 (1976): 1–19.

Weintraub, E. *Microfoundations*. Cambridge: Cambridge University Press, 1979.

Wimsatt, William C. "Reductionism and Its Heuristics: Making Methodological Reductionism Honest." *Synthese*, 2006.

Index

A
actor-centered sociology, 3, 7, 8, 14, 32, 44, 47, 51, 53, 54, 73, 75, 84, 161–163
Affordable Care Act, 6, 127, 129
agencies, 4, 5, 7, 14, 40, 41, 44, 45, 58, 59, 61–63, 88, 91, 92, 94, 95, 98, 99, 102, 105–107, 126, 127, 130, 131, 133, 142, 146, 147, 149, 152, 153, 161–163
assemblages, 5, 59–61, 161, 162
audit, 39, 104, 106, 159
authority, 3, 4, 12, 20, 36, 38, 59, 72, 73, 97–99, 104, 107, 125, 126, 131, 149, 156, 161–163

B
Boeing 737 MAX, 94, 149
bounded rationality, 10, 56
bureaucracy, 63, 64, 113, 126

C
capitalism, 28, 62
causal mechanisms, 2, 18–21, 23–29, 42–44, 48, 51, 61, 63, 67, 73–77, 79, 80, 83, 85, 86, 92, 102–104, 117–120, 129, 139, 147, 150, 159, 161, 162, 164
causal powers, 2, 8, 17, 21, 23, 24, 35, 36, 93
causal substrate, 29
causation, 21, 23, 24, 26–29, 42, 61, 86
Chernobyl, 81, 94
class, 19, 20, 27, 62, 63, 120
class conflict, 5, 20
climate change, 5, 55, 130, 139
collective actors, 88
common-property resource regime, 56, 74
communication, 4, 9, 12, 13, 20, 49, 85, 87, 93, 95, 98, 99, 104, 105, 159, 162, 163

conflict of interest, 72, 92, 100, 101, 104–106, 150, 152
Congress, 5, 7, 22, 117, 131, 141, 150, 154, 155
contentious politics, 87, 88
contingency, 3, 5, 32, 46, 48, 50, 55, 59, 60, 128, 130
conventions, 37, 54
coordination, 3, 4, 12, 13, 59, 74, 85, 88, 93, 98–100, 105, 107, 162, 163
co-regulation, 155–158
corporations, 7, 14, 63, 67, 68, 82, 102, 113, 121, 126, 130, 131, 133, 135, 136, 142, 143, 146, 148, 149, 163
corruption, 82, 92, 93, 102–104, 114, 121, 152
culture, 10, 11, 14, 17, 20, 22, 30, 38, 39, 45, 50, 54–57, 71, 72, 75, 80–83, 95, 101, 103, 104, 117, 121, 130, 154, 155, 161, 162, 164

D
DDT, 133, 138
democracy, 29, 48, 63, 64, 66, 111–118, 121, 122, 151, 155, 162
democratic theory, 66, 112, 116
dysfunction, 2, 5, 13, 42, 92, 95, 96, 102, 103, 106, 107, 164

E
economic interests, 62, 63, 98, 134, 138, 142, 150, 151, 153
economic power, 63, 64, 149
embeddedness, 38, 39
emergence, 6, 8, 31, 40–44, 64, 79, 114, 130
empiricism, 23

environment, 5, 6, 55, 57, 129, 136, 138–141, 148, 152, 157, 158
environmental legislation, 6, 127, 136
Environmental Protection Agency, 4, 7, 131, 136, 147

F
free-riders, 28
Fukushima, 94, 153, 154
functionalism, 10
functional properties, 3, 11, 99, 125, 126

G
GAO, 106, 154
generativism, 5, 41, 44
government, 17, 91, 125, 161

H
healthcare, 6, 104, 127, 128, 143
heterogeneity, 3, 32, 36, 45, 46, 48, 49, 60, 61, 76
high-reliability oganization, 106

I
ideology, 20, 23, 49, 63, 65, 67, 129, 139, 141, 150, 154
incentives, 2, 9, 10, 12, 14, 30, 38, 54, 67, 71, 72, 78, 82, 102, 103, 122
influence, 2, 21, 26, 50, 59, 62–68, 86, 88, 92, 94, 95, 104, 111–113, 118, 128, 129, 132, 133, 135, 136, 141–143, 146, 148–150, 152–155, 159, 161–163
institutions, 2, 3, 5–8, 17, 20–23, 25, 26, 28, 29, 35, 36, 38–43, 45–48, 54, 56–58, 63–65, 67,

68, 72–76, 79, 80, 82, 93, 95, 102, 103, 106, 111–115, 119, 121, 122, 130, 133, 134, 146, 152, 156–158, 161–163
internal governance units, 59, 73

L
labor market, 72
laws, 6, 25, 49, 68, 112, 128
leadership, 12, 13, 81–83, 104, 130
legislation, 4, 5, 7, 63, 64, 107, 112, 113, 117, 119, 127–129, 132, 136, 137, 141–143, 150, 158
liquid modernity, 47
loose coupling, 91, 92, 96, 98–100, 105

M
marginality, social, 121
meso-level, 9, 20, 23, 43–45, 58
methodological individualism, 8, 31, 36, 37, 43, 44
methodological localism, 8, 29
microfoundations, 8, 27, 30, 36, 37, 44, 45, 73, 79
mobilization, 84–88, 116, 118, 119
morphogenesis, 30–32, 40

N
natural sciences, 2, 18, 20
natural systems, 55, 56, 92
network theory, 84, 87
new institutionalism, 28, 73, 74
normative system, 17, 20, 25, 35–39, 45, 71, 72, 76, 77, 79, 93, 114
norms, 2, 3, 8, 9, 11, 21, 30–32, 37, 39, 40, 56, 57, 61, 71–74, 76–81, 93, 162
Nuclear Regulatory Commission, 3, 4, 92, 93, 96, 147, 152–155

O
ontological individualism, 8, 36, 37
ontology, 2, 3, 5, 7, 13, 17–22, 24, 27–30, 32, 35–37, 39, 44, 45, 51, 53–59, 61–64, 72, 73, 84, 85, 88, 93, 107, 111, 112, 122, 125, 126, 136, 138, 147, 159, 161–163
open-system, 5, 56, 57, 147
organizational behavior, 10, 11, 13, 55–57, 79, 103, 140, 162
organizational theory, 10, 11, 56, 57, 75
organizations, 3–5, 7, 9–14, 17, 20, 21, 23, 35, 36, 38–48, 53–60, 68, 73, 75, 79–85, 87, 88, 91–107, 117, 118, 120, 122, 125, 126, 131, 133, 142, 143, 146, 147, 150, 151, 156, 157, 159, 161–164
organization(s), social, 2, 44, 46, 107

P
plasticity, 2, 36, 45, 46, 48, 59
policies, 3–7, 57, 75, 94, 101, 106, 112, 120, 121, 126, 127, 130, 131, 134, 136, 139, 146, 159, 162, 163
political power, 25, 63, 65, 74, 111, 113, 149, 154
populism, 26, 118, 120
positivism, 2
power, 3, 11, 12, 19, 32, 35, 36, 38, 58, 63–68, 73, 75, 88, 94, 102, 104, 111, 113–115, 130, 136, 150, 151, 154, 155, 162, 163
power elite, 67, 68
powerful outsiders, 94, 112, 126, 139, 141, 142, 148, 152, 163
pragmatism, 115
President, 3, 4, 6, 126–128, 136, 142, 152

principal-agent problem, 12, 74, 92, 97, 98, 103–105, 145, 146, 163
public administration, 2, 4, 21, 36, 53, 54, 64, 105
public good, 6, 20, 96, 147, 163, 164
public interest, 20, 106, 139, 151
public opinion, 5, 55, 122, 129, 141, 151

Q
quiet politics, 63

R
realism, 17, 18, 20–23
realism, critical, 23–26, 30
realism, scientific, 18, 19, 21, 23, 26
reductionism, 8, 41, 43, 44, 94, 104
regulation, 2, 64, 86, 101, 107, 113, 140, 142, 145–152, 154–158, 161, 162
regulation, delegated, 149, 150, 157
regulators, 95, 147, 148, 153, 156
regulatory oversight, 149, 150
regulatory systems, 149, 151, 155
relative explanatory autonomy, 40, 43, 44
risk, 7, 22, 94, 139, 140, 154, 158
roles, 3, 5, 9, 11, 12, 39, 47, 48, 53, 55, 58, 59, 71–73, 91, 94, 100, 131, 136, 149, 162

S
safety-case regime, 158
science, 136, 139

scientific assessment, 133
scientific experts, 134
self-regulation, 151, 155–157
social actor, 17, 20, 30, 37, 38, 75, 76
social capital, 67, 84–86
social entities, 2, 6, 8, 18, 19, 21–23, 25, 30, 36, 39, 44–48, 61, 71, 72, 93
social identity, 25, 26
social movements, 48, 58, 116, 117, 122, 129
social networks, 14, 17, 20, 22, 35, 36, 38, 39, 55, 67, 72, 84–86, 88, 161, 162
social structures, 9, 19, 20, 23, 25, 26, 31, 32, 35–37, 39, 44, 47, 48, 58, 59, 68, 72, 87
strategic action fields, 56–58, 73, 75, 93, 95, 96, 147
supervenience, 41
supervision, 12, 74, 95, 103

T
technological innovation, 5, 55
technology policy, 133, 139
Three Mile Island, 81, 94
trust, 13, 20, 38, 119, 121

U
uncertainty, 7, 134

W
War on Poverty, 6, 127

CPSIA information can be obtained
at www.ICGtesting.com
Printed in the USA
LVHW111442120720
660448LV00011B/642